The Saving Mysteries
of Jesus Christ

*W*esleyan Doctrine Series

The Wesleyan Doctrine Series seeks to reintroduce Christians in the Wesleyan tradition to the beauty of doctrine. The volumes in the series draw on the key sources for Wesleyan teaching: Scripture, Liturgy, Hymnody, the General Rules, the Articles of Religion and various Confessions. In this sense, it seeks to be distinctively Wesleyan. But it does this with a profound interest and respect for the unity and catholicity of Christ's body, the church, which is also distinctly Wesleyan. For this reason, the series supplements the Wesleyan tradition with the gifts of the church catholic, ancient, and contemporary. The Wesleyan tradition cannot survive without a genuine "Catholic Spirit." These volumes are intended for laity who have a holy desire to understand the faith they received at their baptism.

EDITORS:
Randy Cooper
Andrew Kinsey
D. Brent Laytham
D. Stephen Long

The Saving Mysteries of Jesus Christ

A Christology in the Wesleyan Tradition

EDGARDO COLÓN-EMERIC
and MARK GORMAN

With Questions for Consideration by Andrew Kinsey

CASCADE *Books* · Eugene, Oregon

THE SAVING MYSTERIES OF JESUS CHRIST
A Christology in the Wesleyan Tradition

Wesleyan Doctrine Series 4

Cascade Books
An Imprint of Wipf and Stock Publishers
199 W. 8th Ave., Suite 3
Eugene, OR 97401

www.wipfandstock.com

PAPERBACK ISBN: 978-1-5326-7606-2
HARDCOVER ISBN: 978-1-5326-7607-9
EBOOK ISBN: 978-1-5326-7608-6

Cataloguing-in-Publication data:

Names: Colón-Emeric, Edgardo Antonio, 1968–, author. | Gorman, Mark, author. | Kinsey, Andrew, author.

Title: The saving mysteries of Jesus Christ : a christology in the Wesleyan tradition / Edgardo Colón-Emeric and Mark Gorman ; questions for consideration by Andrew Kinsey.

Description: Eugene, OR : Cascade Books, 2019 | Series: Wesleyan Doctrine 4 | Includes bibliographical references.

Identifiers: ISBN 978-1-5326-7606-2 (paperback) | ISBN 978-1-5326-7607-9 (hardcover) | ISBN 978-1-5326-7608-6 (ebook)

Subjects: LCSH: Jesus Christ—History of doctrines—18th century. | Wesley, John,— 1703–1791—Contributions in Christology. | Christology. | Methodist Church—Doctrines. | Theology. | Theology, doctrinal.

Classification: BT198 .C60 2019 (paperback) | BT198 .C60 (ebook)

Manufactured in the U.S.A.   08/28/19

Contents

Comments and Questions

Edgardo Colón-Emeric and Mark Gorman's volume on christology in the Wesleyan Doctrine Series provides a wonderful opportunity to explore the person and work of Jesus Christ. It affords the church insight into the mystery or mysteries of Christ and into the ways Christians may participate in that mystery. There are plenty of insights here to engage persons and groups in the life of the church, even outside the church.

The Questions for Consideration at the end of the chapters are meant to assist readers in investigating the importance of Christian doctrine, in this case, the importance of the mystery of who Christ is and what Christ has done. To be sure, they do not exhaust all the angles of the present subject, but rather provide signposts for ongoing reflection. The current set of questions will hopefully help to supply encouragement to those whose own souls seek the vitality of deep knowledge and faithful piety, joined together in Christ.

Introduction

Christology (literally, "a word about Christ") is the branch of Christian doctrine specifically concerning the person and work of Jesus Christ. The introductions of many works on Christian doctrine and belief begin with "this area of our faith is rarely discussed and needs more attention," or something very similar. You see this kind of thing especially in books on the Trinity.

But in this case nothing could be further from the truth. There are plenty of books and other resources about Jesus. We are told we live in a post-Christian era, but popular-level articles about the life of Jesus are still annual fare near Eastertime. Films depicting Christ, whether in the theater or on television, still draw large audiences. Even archaeological discoveries end up in news headlines when they concern events related to Jesus. With all of this, why does the church need another book on christology?

Well, we believe that producing large amounts of material about Jesus is not the same thing as saying something significant about who Jesus is and why he matters. There is much babbling about Jesus, but there is still very little wisdom about him. We hope, in this book, to tap into one vein of wisdom concerning Christ: the saving mystery of Jesus Christ. Though fairly common within the broad Christian tradition, the word "mystery" is not one Methodists, or other Wesleyan Christians, use frequently (we'll say more about this word in the pages below). So we write about the mystery of Christ first of all in order to offer those, like us, within the Wesleyan tradition a way of reflecting on the person and work of Jesus Christ that is both new and recognizably rooted in the tradition of our faith. We also write, however, believing that the Wesleyan ways in which we approach the mystery of Christ can benefit readers regardless of their denominational affiliations or backgrounds.

Methodists and Christology

Methodists, or, more broadly, Wesleyans, do not have distinctive beliefs about Jesus Christ that are fundamentally different from those of the Roman Catholic, Eastern Orthodox, Baptist, Presbyterian, or other Christian traditions. As Ted Campbell says, "What Methodist doctrine teaches about the worship of the Trinity, the nature of Christ, and the Holy Spirit is consonant with the faith of the historic Christian community."[1] United Methodist doctrines about Christ, for example, affirm historic Christian language about Christ being the Son or Word of God; the two natures (human and divine) of Christ; Christ's birth from the Virgin Mary; Christ's real suffering and actual death; and the resurrection and ascension of Christ.[2]

On the whole, however, Methodists have tended to dwell less on the *person* of Christ and emphasize more the *work* of Christ. This does not mean that we are not interested in who Jesus is, but it does mean that, historically, we have underscored Jesus's importance through words like Savior and Redeemer.

What about the founding brothers of Methodism, John and Charles Wesley? First off, it must be said that Methodists come by our interest in the work of Christ honestly. Both Wesleys "published abroad" the saving work of Christ as they preached revival in the eighteenth century. Neither John Wesley nor Charles Wesley wrote a treatise on christology. Their sermons tend to be more concerned with salvation than doctrinal issues about the person of Christ, though there are some exceptions.[3] Interestingly, we have no sermons from either Wesley for Christmas, often a time to reflect on who it is that has come to save us at this Feast of the Incarnation.

To complicate matters further, some scholars have accused John Wesley of practical monophysitism or practical Arianism. That is, these scholars believe that Wesley's sermons and other works do not convey

---

1. Campbell, *Methodist Doctrine*, 48.

2. See "The Articles of Religion" and "The Confession of Faith," in *Book of Discipline*, 104.

3. For example, J. Wesley, "Spiritual Worship."

well that Christ is two natures (monophysitism: one nature) or even that they depict Christ as subordinate to or a creation of God the Father (Arianism, named after the fourth-century heretic Arius). We believe, however, that John Wesley had ample opportunities to show his cards as a heterodox Christian in an era that was rife with interest in Arianism, Socinianism, Unitarianism, and Deism.[4] Wesley did not ally himself with these positions and, quite frequently, rejected their hold on English theological discourse in the eighteenth century.

One of the best and most comprehensive examples of the Wesleys' christological commitments is the *Nativity Hymns* (1745). This theologically rich collection of poetry does reveal a deeper Wesleyan interest in who Christ is, and it is a shame that most contemporary Methodists likely know only one of the *Nativity Hymns* (Hymn 10, "Come Thou Long-Expected Jesus"). Jason Vickers has identified three major themes that run through this collection: doxology, or praise of God for Christ; salvation and deification, or our hope for growing in Christlikeness; and the mystery of Christ's birth and the limits of human understanding.[5]

It is this notion of mystery that especially interests us. John Wesley demonstrates his familiarity and comfort with the theme of the saving mystery of Christ not only in the *Nativity Hymns* but also in the *Sunday Service*. The *Sunday Service* was Wesley's adaptation of the *Book of Common Prayer* of the Church of England, which he prepared for American Methodists following the Revolutionary War. One of the longer prayers Wesley included in the *Sunday Service*, actually intended to be used on Wednesdays and Fridays, was a litany of some forty petitions. The first few petitions are praises to the Triune God; following these are supplications for deliverance, first for deliverance *from* certain sins and evils and, then, deliverance *by* key aspects of the life of Jesus Christ. Here are the relevant petitions:

> By the mystery of thy holy Incarnation; by thy holy Nativity and Circumcision; by thy Baptism, Fasting and Temptation,

---

4. Arianism, as already mentioned, argues that the Son is subordinate to or a creature of the Father. Similarly, Socinianism, which emerged in the Reformation era, argues that Christ came into being only at his birth and so rejects the preexisting divine nature of Christ. Unitarianism rejects the doctrine of the Trinity in favor of a unitary, singular godhead. Deism, emerging from Enlightenment-era rationalism, allows that a god exists but denies god's involvement within creation once the initial act of creation was completed.

5. Vickers, "Charles Wesley's Hymns."

Good Lord, deliver us.

By thine Agony and bloody Sweat; by thy Cross and Passion; by thy precious Death and Burial; by thy glorious Resurrection and Ascension; and by the coming of the Holy Ghost,

Good Lord, deliver us.

These petitions are a liturgical reminder that the *whole* of Christ's life is the source of Christian hope and salvation, which are sometimes restricted to the events of the passion and resurrection.

Although there are only two responses, we can actually divide this section of the litany into eight petitions: (1) the Mystery of the Incarnation; (2) the Nativity and Circumcision; (3) Baptism, Fasting, and Temptation; (4) Agony and Bloody Sweat; (5) Cross and Passion; (6) Death and Burial; (7) Resurrection and Ascension; and (8) the Coming of the Holy Ghost. The heading we might apply to these petitions is found in the first one: "the Mystery of the Incarnation." Each of the remaining seven prayers invokes an event or stage or mystery that follows from this initial "mystery."

It is these eight mysteries, which comprise the saving mystery of Jesus Christ, that we will address and explore in this volume of christology. But to call these mysteries raises an obvious question: what do we mean by "mystery"?

Mysteries and the Mystery of Christ

In our age, the word "mystery" is most often a synonym for "puzzle." A mystery is something that a clever or cunning person (a detective) sets about to solve. Who murdered the duchess? How did they escape? What really happened in the dining room that night? These are the kinds of mysteries we tend to hear about these days.

Contained in this contemporary idea of mystery is the notion that a mystery is something shrouded in secrecy, knowledge of which is not readily available to just anyone. And this notion of secrecy and hidden knowledge is not too distant from the roots of the word "mystery" itself, which comes from the ancient Greek verb *múein*, "to close," as in a closed mouth. In the Hellenistic world, mystery cults were secretive religious societies that practiced various rites. In these rites the people were participants in the events of the god who was cultically represented. These rites offered the gift of salvation. To participate in them required

induction through special initiation rituals; the uninitiated were excluded. The point was not to solve a riddle or a puzzle but to participate in
these hidden ritual celebrations of the mysteries. Cult members took a
vow of silence regarding the rites and the events they portrayed. Hence
the word *múein*.

Although "mystery" has its roots in Hellenist culture, *múein* and
related terms like *mystérion* are also found in the Christian Scriptures.
In the Septuagint, the Greek version of the Old Testament, in the book
of Daniel, "mystery" adopts an eschatological and even apocalyptic con-
notation similar to that found later among gnostic groups. The term
increases in prominence in the New Testament, where, for example, the
Gospels speak of the revealed mysteries of the kingdom of God: revealed
in the person of Jesus Christ. In Mark 4:11, for instance, Jesus says to
his disciples, "To you has been given the secret of the kingdom of God,
but for those outside, everything comes in parables."[6] Here the disciples
are addressed like the initiates of a mystery cult, access to which is made
more difficult by the parables Jesus tells to "outsiders."

The Apostle Paul speaks more generally of the mystery of Christ.
This mystery is disclosed in the events of the passion and exaltation of
Christ (sometimes called the *kerygma*, or emerging Christian preaching). In this mystery, the new age breaks in upon the old, so its content
includes consequences rooted in the *kerygma*, some of which are para-
doxical. Paul addresses the mystery of "the hardening of Israel" and the
welcome of gentiles to the benefits of God's salvation (Rom 11:25; also
Eph 1:9; 3:3); the mystery of the resurrection (1 Cor 15:51); the mystery
of sin (2 Thess 2:7); and the mystery of the Gospel itself (1 Tim 3:16). In
distinction from the practice of the Hellenistic mystery cults, witness to
the saving power of the mysteries of Christ came by becoming servants
of the Gospel, as Paul had done (1 Cor 4:1), and by disclosing the mysteries of Christ in terms and acts that were accessible, not cloaking them
in hazy, sophomoric rhetoric (1 Cor 2:1). The ultimate display of these
mysteries is not in the mastery of secret or prophetic knowledge but in
acts of love (1 Cor 13:2).

After the apostolic age, the term "mystery" seems to have fallen out
of favor among Christians for some time, but it returns with the emer-
gence of the gnostics, who prized specialized and occult knowledge.
Against the gnostics, Christians, especially from the Alexandrian school

6. All Scripture passages are taken from the NRSV.

of theology, reintroduced the term to claim Christianity as the true mystery cult, with Christ as the *mystagogue*, or the one who leads initiates in the rituals of the mystery of salvation. Along the same lines, then, the mysteries became associated with what we now call the sacraments (Latin-speaking Christians used *sacramentum*, the word for an oath taken by a Roman soldier, to translate Greek words for mystery), and *mystagogy* became the term for teaching about the significance of baptism and the Eucharist.

In this book, we draw principally on the sense of mystery used by the litany of the *Sunday Service*, the Gospels, and the Apostle Paul in reference to the salvific importance of the full range of the events of the incarnation. The mystery of the person of Jesus Christ is that his whole life is "for us and for our salvation," as we confess in the Nicene Creed. We reflect on this mystery by considering each of the eight mysteries introduced above (xi–xii). Beginning with chapter 2, we address each saving mystery in a separate chapter, with the exception of "Death and Burial," which we discuss at the beginning of chapter 7.

But we never lose sight of the element of participation that is so central to the way *mystery* has been used. This book began as lectures for an introduction to Christian theology course taught by Edgardo Colón-Emeric at Duke Divinity School. That course emphasized that participation is actually central to true appreciation of the mystery of Jesus Christ, and participation comes in several forms. Participation comes as doxology, or offering praise to God for all aspects of Christ's saving life. It also comes as seeing the elements of the mystery of Jesus Christ as examples or a form of life for us to follow, in order to enjoy the benefits of Christ's salvation. We will offer comments on these aspects of the mystery of Jesus Christ from time to time through the following chapters, and we will also close the book with a final chapter on what it means to confess the mystery of Jesus Christ. Each chapter also has a stanza or two from a hymn (a form of doxology) and opens with a brief discussion of the chapter's hymn.

Finally, we do not want to give the impression that each of these eight saving mysteries is a discrete object in its own right, independent from the others. So we open with a chapter on the person of Jesus Christ. Just as Jesus Christ unifies the two natures, human and divine, in one person, so he also unifies these eight mysteries in a single mystery of salvation.

Questions for Consideration:

1. What is christology?

2. How may focusing on the mystery of Jesus Christ help Christians from a wide variety of backgrounds come to terms with the person and work of Christ?

3. Why is the element of participation so central to the way we may know Christ, in forms of worship and praise and in forms of service and devotion?

4. How may Methodists, or Wesleyans more broadly, speak of the eight saving mysteries of Jesus Christ? That is, may speaking of mystery in the Wesleyan-Methodist theological tradition seem counter to an activist notion of faith and life?

one

The Person of Christ

True God of true God,
Light from Light Eternal,
Lo, he shuns not the Virgin's womb;
Son of the Father, begotten, not created;
O Come, let us adore him, Christ the Lord.[1]

For many Christians, it is hard to imagine a Christmas season with-out singing John Wade's "O Come, All Ye Faithful." As with so many beautiful things, however, our familiarity with the hymn, and perhaps our sentimental attachments to it, may cause us to miss the depths of the poetry contained within. This stanza, for example, captures in just a few lines essential components of Christian belief: Christ is "true God," and Christ is "eternal," meaning Christ did not come into being at any point in time. Christ is the "Son" and not a creature. These lines emphasize the divinity of Christ, but hidden within them is the awesome mystery of the incarnation: "Lo, he shuns not the Virgin's womb." Christ is divine, yet Christ is also human. And, as the refrain of the hymn reminds us, our

1. Wade, "Adeste Fideles," *United Methodist Hymnal*, No. 234, stanza 2.

1

calling is not to solve this paradox but to offer our adoration to Christ the Lord.

In Christian theology, "person," historically, has been the word that indicates the unity of the divine and human aspects of Jesus Christ. For centuries the church has wrestled with language for balancing these two aspects and sometimes has struggled with losing sight of one or the other. Our belief in the unified person of Christ rests on two basic affirmations: (1) only God can save us, and (2) God saves us by becoming one of us.

Christological Heresies

Heresy is a fraught word, conjuring images of angry cardinals and book burnings, but beliefs and opinions that have been rejected over the centuries by the church can help us better understand the affirmations the church has made concerning Christ. Three christological heresies—Arianism, Docetism, and Adoptionism—are particularly useful. Arianism adopts one position, Docetism is its polar opposite, and Adoptionism is a midpoint between the two.[2]

Arianism, named after the fourth-century bishop Arius (and perhaps not actually a belief that he espoused), denies the full divinity of Christ. Its namesake is purported to have said of Christ, "There was a time when he was not," which stands as a rejection of an eternal divine nature being essential to who Jesus Christ is. The most radical versions of Arianism, which continues to have irregular periods of popularity among some theologians, reject Christ's divinity altogether. In some forms of this rejection, Christ is simply an admirable human being, a good example for us to follow. In other forms, Christ belongs to a sub-order of divinity, a demigod of sorts.

Docetism, on the other hand, has trouble with Jesus's humanity. The word itself comes from the Greek word *dokeo*, which means "to seem" or "to appear." The Docetic Christ appears to be a human being, but in reality he is not. He was not really born, and he did not really die. Some Docetists believed that the divine nature would never permit itself to be polluted by real contact with the far-inferior human nature. Others were

---

2. To be clear, we are not saying this is how these heresies developed historically. We are only saying that this is how they map in relation to each other, outside of their original historical contexts.

uncomfortable with associating divinity with death or with a woman's body in a real birth.

Adoptionism finds itself somewhere between Arianism and Docetism. Adoptionists argue that Christ *became* divine at some point along the way in his life—but not at his birth. Common details within the narrative of Christ's life for identifying that point include the baptism of Christ in the Jordan River by John the Baptist; Christ's transfiguration on the mountaintop, with Moses and Elijah present; and Christ's resurrection from the dead.

What Arianism, Docetism, and Adoptionism all have in common is a high level of discomfort with the idea that divinity and humanity would ever come into full contact with each other. The idea that divinity and humanity could really unite is too extreme for all three heresies. Arianism seeks to retreat from that extreme position by downplaying Christ's divinity, Docetism by downplaying Christ's humanity, and Adoptionism by narrowing the scope of the divine-human relationship.

Yet the church decided to adopt precisely this extreme position:[3] that Jesus Christ is truly and fully God and truly and fully human, united in one person. Keeping these two together has not always been easy, and for clarity's sake we will examine the divinity and the humanity of Christ separately before concluding with the unity of the person of Christ.

The Divinity of Christ

Two key words signify the divine nature of Jesus Christ: Son and Word. Of the two, "Son" has a slightly more complicated explanation. In the Scriptures, "Son," whether "Son of Man" or even "Son of God," is not always used in situations that directly connect to Jesus Christ. Both appear in the Old Testament, in Daniel and in Psalms, and both leave open the possibility of referring to someone other than Christ. For example, the psalmist writes, "I will tell of the decree of the LORD: He said to me, 'You are my son; today I have begotten you'" (Ps 2:7). In the context, the recipient of the title "son" is likely an inheritor of the Davidic throne, and being called a "son" is a way of saying the king is specially chosen or blessed. In the New Testament, however, the word Son, and especially the term "Son of God," begin to mean something much more significant than specially chosen or blessed. It is how Satan addresses Jesus (Matt 4) and what the

---

3. Byassee, *Trinity*, 17.

disciples call him when they "worshiped him" after the calming of the sea (Matt 14:33). All four Gospels refer to Jesus as the Son of God; in Luke's Gospel, the title first arises in the context of a special birth enabled by the power of the Holy Spirit (Luke 1:35). Outside the Gospels, the use of "Son of God" amplifies the implication that the relationship of Christ to God is uniquely special. Eventually, the church learned to articulate more clearly that the relationship of "Son" was not a temporal relationship at all. The relationship of God the Father to "the Son" did not begin at the birth, or even the conception, of Jesus. Instead, the Son is "eternally begotten of the Father, God from God, light from light, true God from true God, begotten, not made," as the Nicene Creed professes.

One of the reasons the church articulated this eternal Sonship was due to the significance of the title "Word" in the first chapter of John's Gospel. John writes, "In the beginning was the Word, and the Word was with God, and the Word was God. He was with God in the beginning. All things came into being through him, and without him not one thing came into being" (John 1:1–3). Two extraordinary claims are made here: first, that "the Word" is identifiable with and yet distinguishable from God ("In the beginning . . . the Word was God"); second, that "the Word" does not "come into being." The Word is fully God, not a demigod or a creature.

The church, and indeed the Gospel of John, saw that "Son of God" and "Word" are not merely different, unrelated titles for Jesus Christ. They are synonyms. So if "the Word" exists eternally, so too does "the Son." From here, also, the church's speech concerning the Trinity developed, exploring especially the relational implications of the language of "Father" and "Son," as well as "Holy Spirit," in order to say how the Word/Son could exist eternally as God without there being two gods.

In his sermon "Spiritual Worship," John Wesley draws on another Johannine verse, 1 John 5:20, in order to emphasize that the Son of God is not just "really God" but is actually "the true God": "in glory equal with the Father, in majesty coeternal."[4] Wesley lists seven roles that belong exclusively to God and explains, briefly, how each applies to Christ: Creator, Supporter, Preserver, Author, Redeemer, Governor, and End. Significantly, only one of these roles ("Redeemer") has to do with the history of salvation in the God-man Jesus Christ. So for Wesley, and the church catholic, to confess that the Son of God is true God implicates the

---

4. J. Wesley, "Spiritual Worship," 1.1.

Son fully in the entire range of divine activities with respect to the created world. The Son is, with the Father and the Spirit, co-involved at each point of contact between God and the universe God has made.

Another way of putting all of this is to say that the Son is *by nature* God. At the same time, the testimony of Scripture to the revelation of God the Son is not about a voice speaking through the fire of a burning bush; it is about a character named Jesus who embodies this divine Sonship on earth. To say that Jesus Christ is fully divine attests to only part of the divine revelation of the Son.

The Humanity of Christ

Athanasius of Alexandria, one of the most outspoken voices in the fourth-century christological debates, famously wrote, "The Son of God became human that we might become God." In our era of often-rabid interest in the "historical Jesus," it is hard to imagine that the humanity of Christ could ever be a stumbling block: of course Jesus was fully human! What else could he have been?

As we suggested in our discussion of Arianism, Docetism, and Adoptionism, however, Jesus's humanity was a problem for many people in the ancient world. Even today, among many believers, there can be discomfort with discussing the "full" humanity of Jesus: his need for sleep, for example, or whether he had aches and pains, or what he looked like.

It is important to affirm, whenever possible, that Jesus had—indeed, after the resurrection, still has—a real human body. That body was subject to change and growth and pain and loss, just like every other human body. Six of the seven mysteries of Christ we discuss in this book directly implicate the body of Christ. The heart of Christian belief about the humanity of Christ, though, features a much bolder claim than "the Son of God had a human body." That claim, as important as it is, could leave us with the impression that the divine nature was a puppeteer, with the body of Jesus merely a very realistic puppet (shades of Docetism, to be sure).

Rather, the Christian claim is that Jesus Christ is truly human. Or, as we concluded in the previous section, just as Christ is by nature God, so, too, Christ is *by nature* human. What does it mean to be human by nature? Simply put, it means that whatever all human beings have in common, Christ is these things, too. Christ has a human body, as all human beings do. Christ also has a human soul, as all human beings do.

What about human limitations, like sin and ignorance? When John Wesley adapted the Articles of Religion of the Church of England for his American Methodists, he omitted Article XV, "Of Christ alone without Sin." This omission was because Wesley wanted to preserve, through the doctrine of Christian perfection, the possibility that Christians could reach a state of sinless perfection, not because Wesley believed Christ sinned. There are several ways of understanding the sinlessness of Christ. One is to suggest that Christ took upon himself incorrupt human nature, humanity as it was meant to be lived. Another is to suppose that the incarnation divinized human nature; Jesus took upon himself sinful human nature but through the superabundance of divine grace did not sin.

As far as ignorance and other "natural" human limitations are concerned, the biblical evidence is quite compelling. Jesus does not have unlimited physical or intellectual abilities. Prior to the resurrection, he certainly does exhibit certain deeds of power through his body, from walking across the Sea of Galilee in various accounts to passing through the crowds unharmed in Luke 4. The Gospels, however, never suggest that Jesus is Superman, and there is no implication in them that he intuitively knew Einstein's general theory of relativity or the winner of the 1983 Major League Baseball World Series. In fact, Jesus even confesses ignorance of certain things we might otherwise reasonably expect him to know, as one truly divine and truly human. In Mark 13:32, Jesus declares that even he has no knowledge of "that day or hour," the day of God's judgment.

To reach this point is to meet the limits of the value of separately examining the divinity and humanity of Christ. We cannot say that the Son, the divine nature, is ignorant of anything that the Father knows and, at the same time, have any integrity in maintaining the true divinity of Christ. When Jesus says he does not know something only God knows, the ignorance is sheer human ignorance. As a human being, Jesus Christ was "no more omniscient than omnipresent,"[5] but as God he knows as one from whom no secrets are hid. And as the perfect union of God and humanity, Christ epitomizes in his person the saving mystery of our faith.

The Divine-Human Person of Christ

The unity of the divine and human natures in Jesus Christ is not the theological equivalent of some mythological portmanteau beast. Christ

---

5. J. Wesley, *Explanatory Notes*, Mark 13:32, 76.

is not a centaur or a werewolf or a griffin; there is a real union in Christ, a personal union, and not merely a pasting together or juxtaposition of divine and human attributes. At the Council of Chalcedon (AD 451), the church formulated this union in the following manner:

> We all with one voice teach the confession of one and the same Son, our Lord Jesus Christ: the same perfect in divinity and perfect in humanity, the same truly God and truly man, of a rational soul and a body; *consubstantial* with the Father as regards his divinity, and the same consubstantial with us as regards his humanity; like us in all respects except for sin; begotten before the ages from the Father as regards his divinity, and in the last days the same for us and for our salvation from Mary, the *virgin God-bearer* [Theotokos] as regards his humanity; one and the same Christ, Son, Lord, only-begotten, acknowledged in *two natures which undergo no confusion, no change, no division, no separation*; at no point was the difference between the natures taken away through the union, but rather the property of both natures is preserved and *comes together into a single person*.[6]

There is much to process in this long sentence, and explaining some of the language would require more historical commentary than would be beneficial at this juncture. Instead, we have highlighted with italics four key points in the passage. First, the Son is "*consubstantial* with the Father as regards his divinity," which is an affirmation of the full and eternal divinity of the Son. Second, Mary is "the *virgin God-bearer* [Theotokos] as regards his humanity." Mary gives birth to Jesus Christ, and his humanity comes from her, but God is held in her womb, too. Third, in Christ there are "*two natures which undergo no confusion, no change, no division, no separation*." The divine and human natures are neither shaken nor stirred. They are not mixed together, nor do they separate like water and oil. And they do not meld, becoming some new, never-before-existing divine-human composite nature.

Fourth, then, the union of the two natures is nevertheless real: they "[*come*] *together into a single person*." Christians affirm the reality of this union in various ways, one of which is to speak of the "communication of attributes (or properties)." Although the *natures* are not mixed together, the divine and human *attributes* are shared. Christ's body, therefore, is God's body; Christ's face, God's face. Likewise, the human nature is divinized, becoming divine, not by nature, but by sharing in the divine

---

6. The Definition of Chalcedon, in Leith, *Creeds of the Churches*, 36.

attributes. Christ becomes immortal, for example. Commenting on John 3:13, John Wesley summarizes nicely the communication of attributes/ properties: "This is a plain instance of what is usually termed the communication of properties between the divine and human nature; whereby what is proper to the divine nature is spoken concerning the human, and what is proper to the human is, as here, spoken of the divine."[7]

We must admit that all of this is a little overwhelming. What are we to do with all this talk of natures, attributes, and union?

First, we should heed the words of Augustine of Hippo: "If you can comprehend it, it is not God."[8] The desire for simplistic, easy-to-grasp explanations of Jesus Christ masks a desire to bring God under our control, and any god under our control cannot be Truly God; it can only be an idol.

Second, we must overcome our fear of silence. Babbling on and on with endlessly intricate explanations of the God-man Jesus Christ is as futile as the desire for simplicity is idolatrous. Faith comes through hearing. Maintaining a reverent silence in the face of this mystery, a silence that stems from the excess of grace, from having too much to say, from beholding too great a light, is a faithful response as we come to know Christ more and more deeply.

Finally, it is not enough to believe that Christ is fully, truly God and fully, truly human. As James warns his first-century audience, "You believe that God is one; you do well. Even the demons believe—and shudder" (Jas 2:19); there is such a thing as devilish orthodoxy. What our Wesleyan heritage and writers like Athanasius, Augustine, and the members of the Council of Chalcedon have in common is a shared belief in a tight connection between theology and the pursuit of faith and godliness.[9] So we end this chapter on the person of Christ where we began, with a hymn:

> Fixed on the Athanasian mound,
> I still require a firmer ground
> My sinking faith to bear:
> I want to feel my soul renewed
> In the similitude of God,
> Jehovah's character.

---

7. J. Wesley, *Explanatory Notes*, John 3:13, 127.

8. Augustine, Sermon 117.3.5.

9. On this connection in the ancient period, see Torrance, *Trinitarian Faith*, 13–46.

My notions true are notions vain;
By them I cannot grace obtain,
   Or saved from sin arise:
Knowledge acquired by books or creeds
My learned self-righteous pride it feeds;
   'Tis love that edifies.[10]

Questions for Consideration

1. What are some of the images the word *heresy* may conjure up? Is this image accurate? What is lost without the notion of heresy?

2. What are three of the primary christological heresies? How do they diminish the mystery of Christ, the union of divinity and humanity?

3. What are the consequences of failing to understand Christ's humanity and divinity?

4. How did the Council of Chalcedon address the unity of Christ's two natures? What key points do we need to keep in mind?

5. What three warnings may we need to keep in mind regarding the talk of natures, attributes, and union?

---

10. C. Wesley, "Thee, Great Tremendous Deity," *Trinity Hymns* (1767), Hymn 19, stanzas 2 and 3.

two

Incarnation

Creator of the stars of night,
    Your people's everlasting light,
O Christ, redeemer of us all,
    We pray you, hear us when we call.
When this old world drew on toward night,
    You came; but not in splendor bright,
Not as a monarch, but the child
    Of Mary, blameless mother mild.[1]

The great wonder of God's love for us is that the Son of God, the source of all being, became a human being, taking on flesh—and not, as this ninth-century hymn says, "in splendor bright" but as "the child / Of Mary." As the hymn hints, and John Wesley says explicitly in his sermon "The End of Christ's Coming," the revelation of the Son in Jesus Christ was not the first manifestation of the Word of God. The unenfleshed Word "was manifested as the only-begotten Son of God, in glory equal with the Father, to the inhabitants of heaven before and at the

1. "Creator of the Stars of Night," *Glory to God*, No. 84.

10

foundation of the world," at the earliest dawn of creation.[2] In that sermon, Wesley goes on to affirm the manifestation of this unenfleshed Word to the Hebrew patriarchs: Enoch, Noah, Abraham, Isaac, Jacob, and even Moses. None of these prior manifestations, however, matches the fullness of the incarnation, the enfleshment of the eternal Word, the Son of God.

The study of the person of Christ in chapter 1 gives us a basic framework for discussing the incarnation, the taking on of flesh by the eternal Son of God. The incarnation is not just for show (Docetism). Neither does it begin at a certain point within the life of Christ (Adoptionism) or impose some state of inferiority upon the Son (Arianism). Rather, the incarnation is the real union of divine and human natures in the person of Jesus Christ (Chalcedonian Definition).

However, the incarnation plunges us into the depths of the mystery of Christ; a basic framework is hardly sufficient, but then, nothing short of giving our lives fully to Jesus Christ is a sufficient response to the incarnation. Even then we can only marvel at the grace that sustains us in that response. In this chapter we focus on just two essential aspects of the incarnation: first, the divine exchange for our salvation and, second, the role of Mary.

The incarnation is a scandalous belief. In the ancient world, the idea that God would deign to become human was laughable and even insulting to the divine nature; many in our world today continue to be so affronted by the Christian claim that God became flesh in Jesus Christ. This is the scandal of the divine exchange for our salvation. Just as infamous two thousand years ago, and perhaps even more so today, is the claim that God did not take on a generic humanity but embraced exclusively the particular Jewish humanity of a child in the lineage of King David. This is the scandal of the role of Mary.

The scandal is not limited to those outside the Christian faith; Christians must avoid sentimentalizing and domesticating beliefs about Jesus Christ that shield us from the sharp edges of the incarnation. We need that scandal, for the scandal of the incarnation is the reality of our salvation.

2. J. Wesley, "End of Christ's Coming," 2.1.

The Miraculous Exchange

When the Word, or Son, of God became flesh and tabernacled with us, as John says in the prologue of his Gospel, it was a stunning moment of cosmic drama. We often use the word "sacrifice" in the context of Jesus Christ and the cross, but already, at the very point of the incarnation, there is an unequal exchange that is impossible to hyperbolize. The Creator of the universe, the one who set the stars in their courses at night, abandons his eternal glory in exchange for the infinitely lesser glory of humankind, creatures of his own making.

Biblical texts, read christologically, consistently reinforce the sacrificial, self-emptying nature of the incarnation itself. The glory of the Creator, for example, is writ large across the Psalms. In Psalm 8, the psalmist sings of the Lord's majesty, of "glory above the heavens" (Ps 8:2) and dares to ask, "What are human beings that you are mindful of them, mortals that you care for them?" (Ps 8:4). The psalmist affirms God's providential care for human beings and expounds on the glory of humankind, but it is a glory under the heavens, not above them, a glory of "things under their feet," not of things above their eyes (Ps 8:6). Similar themes echo through Psalms 19 and 147, among many others. The Lord shows amazing magnanimity and love for creation in giving "the law of the LORD" (Ps 19:7) and in "gather[ing] the outcasts of Israel" (Ps 147:2), but the glory of the Lord shines brightly through the majesty of creation.

Just as surely, the veil of human flesh donned in the incarnation inexplicably hides the divine glory from our sight. Isaiah 53 is often read in Lent or Holy Week, even on Good Friday, but there is no need to wait for the events of the passion and crucifixion of our Lord in order to be in awe of the hidden glory of the Incarnate Christ. "He had no form or majesty that we should look at him," Isaiah writes, "nothing in his appearance that we should desire him" (Isa 53:2). This is the divine exchange: the exchange of "O LORD, our Sovereign, how majestic is your name in all the earth" (Ps 8:1) for "he had no form or majesty that we should look at him." It is of God the Son, the Word who was with God in the beginning, by whom all things were made, that Isaiah dares to say, "We held him of no account" (Isa 53:3).

No biblical text drives home more the sacrificial, self-emptying, *kenotic* (the technical term) nature of the incarnation than Philippians 2:6–11. Sometimes called the Christ Hymn, this great poem, along with John 1, is the New Testament's most significant testimony to the preexistence of Christ, and in it the Apostle Paul frames the life of Christ in terms of an *exitus-reditus* scheme. In this scheme, Christ, "in the form of God . . . [empties] himself" by becoming a human being (the exit or *exitus*); this self-emptying trajectory continues all the way to the cross, which is its nadir, before the turn back or rebound (the *reditus*) occurs when God "has highly exalted him." Worth restating is that in this poem Christ's self-emptying *stops* at the cross, when that work is complete, but begins much earlier, at the point of incarnation.

John Wesley paid careful attention to this passage in his *Notes upon the New Testament*, in which he rehearses some of the very things we have already said concerning this miraculous exchange. Wesley reads Philippians 2:6 as affirming Christ's eternal sharing in "the incommunicable nature of God . . . [in] his own strict and unquestionable right." When Christ enters the world enfleshed as a human being, Wesley says, he does more than hide his glory under a creaturely guise: "Yea, he not only veiled, but, in some sense, renounced, the glory which he had before the world began." This renunciation is a genuinely sacrificial act, a giving up of what Christ had every right to hold in his grasp. And Wesley also invokes, implicitly, Isaiah 53:3 and Psalm 8:1 when he comments upon the humanity that Christ took upon himself as being that of "[a] common man, without any peculiar excellence or comeliness." Christ did not exchange divine glory for human glory as the first-century equivalent of the Sexiest Man Alive. That would be self-renunciation with a wink, a false humility that is merely for show (shades again of Docetism). Christ's humility is genuine, as real as the quite ordinary flesh he bears in ancient Palestine.

So far we have limited our discussion of the miraculous exchange to Christ's exchange of divine glory for creaturely embodiment. This is essential, and it seems to us that we cannot overemphasize it. But it is only one half of the picture. Through this exchange of divinity for humanity, another exchange becomes possible: the elevation of humanity to divinity. Paraphrasing the Nicene Creed just slightly, for us *and for our deification*, the Son of God came down from heaven, was incarnate of the Holy Spirit and the Virgin Mary, and was made truly human.

In modern theology, the language of deification has been seen largely as the vocabulary of the Christian East, the churches of the Orthodox Communion. This language, it is said, is being "recovered" or "rediscovered" in fresh readings of the New Testament, or of Martin Luther, or of

Calvinism by non-Orthodox scholars and theologians of the Christian West, Protestants and Roman Catholics alike.

Wesleyans should especially resonate with this process of recovery or rediscovery, even if the specific language of deification is, at first blush, unfamiliar to us. In fact, much of Wesleyan theology—whether we speak of (in Randy Maddox's phrasing) "responsible grace" or of the intimate connection between justification and sanctification or, certainly, our peculiar doctrine of Christian perfection—rests on the notion that God became a human being in order that human beings might become divine, as Athanasius said in the fourth century. This is the other side of the miraculous exchange.

Charles Wesley helps orient our ideas about the divine exchange toward this notion of deification. Consider the following excerpts from his *Nativity Hymns*:

> He deigns in flesh to appear, / Widest extremes to join, / To bring our vileness near, / And make us all divine; / And we the life of God shall know, / For God is manifest below. (Hymn 5)

> Made flesh for our sake, / That we might partake / The nature divine, / And again, in his image, his holiness shine. (Hymn 8)

> Our Immanuel came, / The whole world to redeem, / And incarnated shewed / That man may again be united to God! (Hymn 14)

> Didst thou not in person join / The natures human and divine, / That God and man might be / Henceforth inseparably one? Haste then and make thy nature known / Incarnated in me. (Hymn 15)

Charles Wesley does not shy away from bold claims and bolder requests in these hymns. In Christ's incarnation God comes to "make us all divine" so "that we might partake / The nature divine." The union of the two natures in Christ presages, for Charles Wesley, a similar union of God and all peoples, so that he even prays, "Haste then, and make thy nature known / Incarnated in me."

Thus the first scandal of the incarnation is the scandal of the divine exchange *for us and for our salvation*. Who dares to say that God became a human being, giving up his glory? Who dares to confess that human beings might share so fully in this exchange that we too, in a very real sense, become divine? It is Christians gathered by the saving mystery of Jesus Christ, the same people who also affirm that this scandal finds its initial resting place in none other than the young Jewish woman Mary, the mother of Jesus Christ, the mother of God.

The Role of Mary

The scandal of the miraculous exchange is matched in intensity perhaps only by the scandal of Mary. Indeed, if anything, Mary deepens the scandal of the miraculous exchange, since, in her, Christians claim that the self-emptying of the Son is not only a stunning theological concept but an actual historical reality, an event of something that has happened within the created time of this world. For while the foundations for the incarnation are laid at the creation of human beings in Genesis 1, the event of the incarnation begins with Mary and the annunciation in Luke 1.

The Feast of the Annunciation (March 25), often overlooked in our Wesleyan tradition, commemorates the extraordinary moment when Mary speaks the holy, "Let it be." This simple phrase harkens back to Genesis 1, when the Lord says of each act of creation, "Let it be." Her words indicate that, as at the earliest moments of the cosmos, a new thing is happening. More than that, her words signify the wondrous particularity of the divine exchange. The Creator God here submits to his creation by yielding himself to *this woman Mary*. God does not submit to the idea of humanity; God exchanges the glory of the Son for the creaturehood of Mary, whose consent is *necessary* for the incarnation. There is no divine imposition of will in this event; there is a real possibility that Mary could have said no to the angel. Her "let it be" is the assent by which the incarnation proceeds within the created order.

How was Mary able to offer her "let it be"? This question vexes, for her faithful and willing answer is distinct in a world where the human tendency is to turn away from God or to issue a "no" to any divine request that may cost us something. In the Roman Catholic tradition, the doctrine of the immaculate conception exempts Mary from the human condition of original sin. In Orthodox thought, Mary's graced answer is the result of a building-up of grace among faithful Israelites over generations. The Reformed answer is to appeal to predestination: Mary's answer was foreordained by the Lord.

Each of these responses offers points of commonality, as well as problems, to those of us in the Wesleyan tradition. We Wesleyans have very little interest in discussing predestination, we generally do not think of grace as something inheritable, and we do not subscribe to the doctrine of the immaculate conception. What we share with those from other traditions, however, is that God is at work in giving Mary the grace to respond with her "let it be," and that God's grace nevertheless does not mean that Mary was a mere automaton in the divine drama. Wesleyans may appeal to a pluriform understanding of grace. Mary's affirmative response to the divine initiative is enabled first by God's prevenient grace, which goes before her and opens paths for her to walk by following the way of the Lord. And as she continues along these paths, sanctifying grace builds up in her over time as she is perfected, becoming more and more like God who made her. In fact, we could say that Mary is the pioneer of Christian perfection. She is the first to reach full perfection in this life in response to the grace of God in Jesus Christ.

The scandal of Mary does not end with the divine self-emptying at the annunciation. Mary is the Blessed Virgin, which is a scandal to many modern ears. Scientists, anthropologists, and scriptural exegetes have all opposed notions of Mary's virginity. Many theologians regard the teaching as unnecessary, seeing her virginity as adding nothing to the event of the incarnation. So many Wesleyans may be surprised to learn that John Wesley not only affirmed that Mary *was* the Blessed Virgin at her son's birth, but he also agreed that Mary *remained* a virgin throughout her life. In his "Letter to a Roman Catholic," Wesley wrote, "I believe that . . . [Christ was] conceived by the singular operation of the Holy Ghost, and born of the blessed Virgin Mary, who, as well after as before she brought Him forth, continued a pure and unspotted virgin."[3] In this, Wesley was consonant with a significant theme that has echoed across the ages of Christianity even to this day, though less frequently in Protestant halls.

Why does it matter whether or not Mary was a virgin? Certainly we allow that the Lord can work however he chooses, and we do not want to impose virginity upon God's actions as a binding necessity. But with Wesley and the Catholic tradition we do affirm the perpetual virginity of Mary. The virgin birth helps mark Christ's incarnation as a unique and extraordinary event; it is an essential sign that in Christ God is doing a new thing. The virgin birth also confirms Mary's faith in the God of Israel and her devotion to her son, our Lord and hers, our Savior and hers. To suggest that Joseph and Mary conceived Jesus together following the annunciation is to have Mary replay the role of Sarah, Abraham's wife, who laughs at God's promises and tries to manipulate her context in order to achieve their fulfillment. But Mary is completely faithful, trusting only in God's grace, not in her own cunning or works. And Mary's devotion to

---

3. J. Wesley, *Works* (Jackson), 10:80–86.

her son, Jesus, is likewise unwavering, a fact underlined by the Gospels, which testify that she accompanied him even to his gruesome crucifixion. He is her only child, though through him she becomes, in a real sense, the mother of all who are members of the body of Christ.

This final point leads us into yet one more scandal of Mary: the scandal of Marian devotion. Mary's unique role in the history of our salvation has been a stumbling block for many over the ages. Protestants have balked at devotion to Mary, preferring iconoclasm, sometimes in severe forms. Scottish Reformer John Knox is reported to have once thrown a statue of the Virgin Mary into the sea. "Let our Lady now save herself," he said. "She is light enough; let her learn to swim!"[4] More recently, a Cuban Methodist was heard to say of a Marian statue, "I want to cut off her head."

On this point neither John nor Charles Wesley is of much help. They mention Mary, the mother of Jesus, infrequently in sermons and hymns (far more common in the hymns is Mary of the sisters Mary and Martha). John Wesley was evidently unconvinced by the honor given Mary by Roman Catholics, believing it was a form of idolatry. Nevertheless, he affirms that she is worthy of Christian honor.

This leaves those of us in the Wesleyan-Methodist heritage with something of a dilemma. On one side, the vitriol of John Knox or the Cuban Methodist is not a legitimate form of honoring the Virgin Mary. On the other side, some (and perhaps all) Roman Catholic practices of Marian devotion seem to be out of bounds. The way forward, we suggest, is to err on the side of honoring Mary. This does not mean we ought to pray to her or ask her to intercede for us. But adopting a tone that is appreciative of her holiness, showing respect for our Lord's mother, and preaching on Mary as an apostle of humility, piety, and Christian perfection are practices to be commended in the place of the divisive Protestant rhetoric that has held sway for far too long. Whatever the historic and theological reasons may be for looking askance at certain Roman Catholic practices, we should not project onto Mary the fractures within the church.

It is also worth bearing in mind that discomfort with Mary's place in christology extends into the past, far beyond the Reformation. As we have already mentioned, at least some of the christological heresies in the first millennium of the church might have been driven in part by an aversion to Mary's *female* body. Not only do we see this in the positions we

4. George, "Blessed Virgin," 100–101, quoted in Anderson, "Mary," 34.

discussed earlier, but it also appears in the context of the debates that led to the Chalcedonian Definition. Nestorius, a bishop whose views were rejected by the Council of Chalcedon, displays some interest in avoiding the claim that God came into contact with Mary's birthing canal. Our point, then, is that when we disregard Mary we find ourselves among uncomfortable historical allies: those who contributed to the bitter Protestant-Catholic divide, early heretics, and anti-female, perhaps even misogynist, men.

Is it not far better to praise and celebrate Mary, and, in the process, find ourselves in the company of proponents of orthodox christology and, indeed, Scripture itself?

In the end, the scandal of the Virgin Mary is the scandal of flesh. Both Scripture and tradition affirm that Mary was a faithful Israelite, a Jew who hewed closely to the covenant given by God. Her son, Jesus, receives his Jewish flesh from her; Mary establishes that Christ is not merely some theological ideal or possibility that God could come to earth. Mary grounds Christ's life in a particular historical reality, on the same plane as the birth of any other child. Further, because Mary was the *theotokos*, the Mother of God, in Jesus Christ the Son of God bore flesh that could grow, age, and even die.

Conclusion

We end this chapter with something hinted at by its opening hymn, "Creator of the Stars of Night." The second stanza begins, "When this old world drew on toward night, / You came; but not in splendor bright." This line recalls Galatians 4:4–5 ("But when the fullness of time had come, God sent his Son, born of a woman, born under the law, in order to redeem those who were under the law, so that we might receive adoption as children") and Hebrews 1:1–2 ("Long ago God spoke to our ancestors in many and various ways by the prophets, but in these last days he has spoken to us by a Son, whom he appointed heir of all things, through whom he also created the worlds"), and it implies an interesting question: why did the incarnation happen *when* it happened?

There is no completely satisfactory answer to this question. The historical answer, from someone like N. T. Wright (who might say, "In order to warn the Jews away from violent rebellion against Rome that would result in the disastrous events of AD 70"), is plausible but incomplete.

Were there not other disasters for the Jews, both prior to and after the destruction of the second temple, where a Messiah would have been of great benefit to God's people? Perhaps, we might add, the timing of Christ's birth only heightens the scandal of the incarnation: Christ came to us through Mary in a period of Palestinian history when almost no one cared about what happened in Palestine.

Of course, we may never know why God chose that particular time. But the timing of Jesus's birth is one of the many particularities of his early life, which is, in its own right, part of the saving mystery of Christ.

Questions for Consideration

1. What is the incarnation?

2. How does the incarnation plunge us into the depths of the mystery of Christ?

3. What is the scandal of the divine exchange between God and humanity that takes place with the incarnation?

4. How may Wesleyans resonate with elements of Eastern Orthodoxy's notion of theosis or deification?

5. How does the role of Mary's consent factor into the mystery of the incarnation?

6. How may Wesleyans understand the scandal of the Virgin Mary in terms of the doctrine of Christian perfection, and how may Wesleyans contribute to larger discussions of Mary among different Christian bodies?

three

Nativity and Circumcision

Glory be to God on high,
    And peace on earth descend;
God comes down: he bows the sky:
    And shews himself our friend!
God th' invisible *appears,*
    God the blest, the great I AM
Sojourns in this vale of tears,
    And Jesus is his name.

Him the angels all ador'd
    Their Maker and their King:
Tidings of their humbled Lord
    They now to mortals bring:
Emptied of his majesty,
    Of his dazzling glories shorn,
Being's source *begins* to be,
    And God himself is BORN!

See th' eternal Son of God
    A mortal Son of man,
Dwelling in an earthy clod
    Whom heaven cannot contain!
Stand amaz'd ye heavens at this!
    See the Lord of earth and skies!
Humbled to the dust he is,
    And in a manger lies![1]

This nativity hymn by Charles Wesley, though less renowned and beloved than "Hark! The Herald Angels Sing," rivals its more famous counterpart in depth and poetry at every point. Wesley's text captures the irresolvable tension that Christians celebrate at Christmas. It is not just a baby who is born at Christmas but, as Wesley says, "God himself." A body now holds him "Whom heaven cannot contain." Most shocking of all: "Being's source *begins* to be."

Elsewhere in the *Nativity Hymns*, Wesley writes of "God contracted to a span."[2] God, who exists outside of time, who is eternal and infinite, is now compressed into the brief span of the lifetime of a single human being, one whose life, even by human standards, is brief and cut short before its time. God, who is not a physical being, whose existence is uncontainable, is now held in the span of the distance from left hand to right hand, from head to toe, of an infant boy. And the contraction of God in the life of this human Jesus anticipates the day when this body and this God will be stretched as far as possible, between two thieves, on the span of the cross.

In this chapter we address the saving mystery of Christ who, in the incarnation, is embodied. The nativity, which nearly all Christians celebrate, and the circumcision of Jesus Christ, which most Christians pass by without noticing, underscore that Christ has a real, human, particular body: one that is able to be born (and so will be able to die); one that enters life as a member of a people with a unique tradition and relationship to God (and so will live out that tradition and relationship uniquely);

1. C. Wesley, "Glory Be to God on High," *Nativity Hymns* (1745), Hymn 4, stanzas 1–3.

2. C. Wesley, "Let Earth and Heaven Combine," *Nativity Hymns* (1745), Hymn 5, stanza 1.

and one that, belonging to that people, is marked through ritual and ceremony as a member (and so will receive new marks in wounds before its death). In treating the well-known side by side with the obscure, we offer a reminder that Christians must remain open to the possibility that every part of Christ's life has significance for our salvation. After we reflect on the nativity and the circumcision of Christ, we will conclude this chapter by touching on the many ways we name the saving union of God and humanity in the one person of Jesus Christ.

Nativity

In chapter 2, we highlighted the scandalous nature of the incarnation. God's decision to become a human being is an affront to human wisdom; the annunciation, not the nativity, is the starting point of that affront within created time. But the birth of Christ is the moment when God's fullest entry into creation becomes, we might say, more than a private affair. Following the annunciation and before the nativity, only a few creatures knew of the coming of Christ. In Luke's Gospel Mary and her cousin Elizabeth (and, arguably, John the Baptist, in utero) both know, and in Matthew's Gospel Joseph knows; these human insiders are complemented by one or two unnamed angels in Matthew and by the angel Gabriel in Luke.

At Jesus's birth, however, the event rapidly becomes more public: shepherds and a host of angels know within hours, possibly, of Christ's birth; Simeon and Anna within a few days; and wise men and Herod within a few years. Jesus's public *ministry* may not begin until he is much older, but starting from the nativity the incarnation becomes a public *event*. It is also an event of cosmic significance; Saint Jerome once said, "Even creation approves our preaching. The universe itself bears witness to the truth of our words. Up to this day the dark days increase, but from this day the darkness decreases."[3] Saint Jerome finds our hope in Christ reflected by the turning of the seasons in our celebration of Christ's nativity.

The nativity of Jesus Christ only heightens the scandalous nature of the incarnation. The birth is a historical event: one that happens within time, at a known place. Luke begins his second chapter, "In those days a decree went out from Emperor Augustus that all the world should be

3. Quoted in Ratzinger, *Spirit of the Liturgy*, 108.

registered. This was the first registration and was taken while Quirinius was governor of Syria" (vv. 1–2). Implicit in these simple verses is that this birth has something in common with other human births: we know, with fair precision, when Christ was born. The events of his birth might be extraordinary, the nature of his birth unique, but the historical fact of his birth is normal, even quotidian. Perhaps ironically, it is precisely the routine, normal fact of this birth that makes it all the more scandalous. God, we believe, really did make a home among mortals. God really chose one time and one place for this spectacular birth over every other time and every other place. God's birth is dateable.

Indeed, once we acknowledge the normalcy of God's birth, the details shock and offend. God was not born in a palace or in great comfort. Christ's nativity takes place in true poverty. He is born in Bethlehem, Beth-Lechem, a town whose name means "house of bread," not "house of luxury" or "house of riches" or even "house of God." Bethlehem—not Rome, not Athens, not even Jerusalem—a tiny hamlet in a backwater province, impossibly irrelevant to the powers of the Roman Empire. And in Bethlehem Christ's birth takes place in a stable, and Mary claims a feeding trough, a manger, for her son's crib. "What a great and marvelous mystery," says the medieval hymn *O magnum mysterium*, "that animals would behold their newborn Lord." This picture does not fit with how our world would anticipate divine entry.

The birth of Christ upends our ideas about poverty and riches. God is found among the poor, with those our world has always accounted as nothing. They receive everything. Shepherds, not rulers, are the first to receive the glad tidings. They run to the stable empty-handed, needing to offer nothing but their worship and praise. The wealthier wise men, in Matthew's Gospel, are the ones who must approach the young child with gifts in hand. The Almighty is cold. The All-Knowing burbles. The creature gives light to the Creator. The Ancient of Days becomes a baby. This is the scandalous poverty of the nativity of Christ.

The birth of Christ is a fulfillment of Scripture. It is not clear who, if anyone, in Israel was expecting a single human Messiah to save God's people by the time Jesus was born. The New Testament writers, however, are the ones who see, in hindsight, the fulfillment of Israel's Scriptures in Jesus Christ. The birth narratives in Matthew and Luke are full of Old Testament references. We do not need to say that Isaiah expected something like what happened to Mary in order to believe that his prophecy "Behold, a virgin shall conceive, and bear a son, and shall call his name

Immanuel" (7:14) or his proclamation "The ox knows its owner, and the donkey its master's crib; but Israel does not know, my people do not understand" (1:3) are brought into their deepest meaning at Christ's birth. The nativity is the birth of God's *novum*, God's new thing in Jesus Christ.

At the nativity we celebrate the Feast of the Incarnation. In his birth Christ graces the birth of all children; in his entry into a human family Christ blesses every human family. And in his poverty Christ opens the way to salvation for all people, a way that begins in lowly Bethlehem and leads to a perverse enthronement in the royal seat of Jerusalem.

Circumcision

As much as we know about Jesus, there remains far more hidden from our sight. Other than a few isolated incidents reported in the Gospels of Matthew and Luke, Jesus's life from infancy until his public ministry is lost to us. Far from being inconsequential, this hidden life is full of meaning. It is a time of human anonymity and divine intimacy; Luke says that Jesus "grew and became strong, filled with wisdom; and the favor of God was upon him" (2:40). It was also a time in which God the Son hallowed the ordinary of life: Jesus, John Wesley suggests, "passed through and sanctified every stage of human life. Old age only did not become him."[4] In this, Christ also models for us "our childhood pattern," in the words of the Victorian Christmas carol "Once in Royal David's City."

Was this period of growth also for Jesus's own benefit? Could Jesus have grown in grace? Could he have grown in wisdom as well as in body? Passages like Matthew 24:36 ("But about that day and hour no one knows, neither the angels of heaven, nor the Son, but only the Father") suggest such growth was not only possible but necessary for Christ, but various theologians have answered the questions differently. Martin Luther affirmed full knowledge, essentially denying the need for growth. Kenotic christologies, which emphasize the self-emptying nature of the incarnation, affirm full ignorance. In between, medieval theologian Thomas Aquinas and twentieth-century theologian Hans Urs von Balthasar have offered creative proposals. Aquinas says that Christ knows fully by divinity and divinized knowledge but not experientially. Balthasar argues that Christ's *mode* of knowing was in waiting on the Father, not grasping the truth to come. John Wesley sees in Christ's early life a model for all

4. J. Wesley, *Explanatory Notes*, Luke 2:43, 87.

Christians, arguing that "though a man were pure, even as Christ was pure, still he would have room to increase in holiness, and, in consequence thereof, to increase in the favour, as well as in the love of God."[5]

Whatever we believe about Christ's *need* for growth, we know from the few details we have about his early life that the time was not spent poorly. In fact, one of the most important and easily overlooked moments in Christ's childhood happened very soon after his birth: his circumcision. This early act marked, quite literally, Jesus's body as that of a Jewish male. We should not pass by this point too quickly. Jesus was born to a Jewish mother and was part of a Jewish household. Joseph and Mary raised him to participate in Jewish religious life, including later pilgrimages to Jerusalem and his circumcision. Far from something imposed upon him by his parents, the Jewishness of Jesus is essential to his identity, and to our salvation through him.

Jesus observed the Sabbath and attended the synagogue regularly (Luke 4). His own self-understanding of his mission on earth was first and foremost as a mission to Jews, a mission "only to the lost sheep of Israel," as he says in rebuking the Canaanite woman's request in Matthew's Gospel (Matt 15:24). He calls "the twelve," a symbolically important number representing the tribes of Israel, and when, in Matthew's Gospel, he sends them out to spread the good news of the kingdom of heaven, he instructs them to avoid gentiles and Samaritans (Matt 10:5). In Luke's Gospel, Jesus sends the seventy, a number that echoes the Septuagint, the name for the Greek translation of the Old Testament, meaning "seventy." Finally, at his crucifixion, he is executed as the "king of the Jews."

In commenting on Jesus's circumcision, John Wesley focused less on Christ's humanity than on his Jewishness. Nevertheless, he sees that Jesus is baptized so "that he might visibly be made under the law by a sacred rite, which obliged him to keep the whole law; as also that he might be owned to be the seed of Abraham, and might put an honour on the solemn dedication of children to God."[6] The circumcision, for Wesley, is part of the public event of the incarnation of Jesus Christ, a making visible of things that are inherently true. Circumcision does not make Jesus Jewish, but it does present him as Jewish. Jesus does not need to found a new community or people because he already had Israel; through Israel Jesus reaches out to all people.

5. J. Wesley, *Explanatory Notes*, Luke 2:52, 87.
6. J. Wesley, *Explanatory Notes*, Luke 2:21, 86.

There is a final word to be said concerning Christ's circumcision: it is the first wound upon Christ's body, but it is not the last. The circumcision foreshadows the crucifixion, when the pagan ritual wounds of execution will further mark the incarnate body of God. Even as an infant, God does not shy away from the painful existence of a fallen creation.

The Names of Jesus

It was no accident that the son of Mary is named Jesus: no accident, because the angel reveals this name to Mary (Luke 1:31). The child will be called Son of the Most High (Luke 1:32), Emmanuel (Matt 1:23), Son of Man, the Holy One of God, Master, Teacher, but his name is Jesus. The name and the purpose, the person and the mission, are inseparable. As the angel tells Joseph, "You are to name him Jesus, for he will save his people from their sins" (Matt 1:21). It is through this child, Jesus, that the saving mysteries of God are revealed in their fullness to the world.

In the early days of Methodism, a woman named Mary Bosanquet (1739–1815) became estranged from her family and joined the Wesleyan movement in London. Eventually, having become, with Sarah Crosby and Sarah Ryan, a leading figure in the movement, Mary Bossanquet received permission to preach among the Methodists. In 1781 she married John Fletcher, John Wesley's protégé, who died in 1785. Twelve years later, she developed a series of reflections on the names of Jesus, which she shared with other Methodists. Mary Bosanquet, now Mary Bosanquet-Fletcher, called these reflections her "Watchwords"; she discussed names and titles like Almighty, babe, bread, dew, eagle, glorious, husband, ladder of Jacob, ointment, rose of Sharon, and tree of life.[7] In the spirit of this sophisticated early Methodist theologian and preacher, we believe it is fitting to close this chapter on Christ's early life with a few thoughts concerning certain names and titles for the one who "will save his people from their sins." We will consider six names or titles: Christ, Logos, Son, Image, God, and Lord.

The name Christ underscores the Jewish hope represented in the life of Jesus. Christ, *christos*, translates the Hebrew word *masiach*, or messiah, which means someone anointed by the Lord to accomplish great things on behalf of God's people. Jesus was hardly the first messiah in Israel's history, and he did not prove to be the last. Yet in his role as "the Christ"

7. See Bosanquet-Fletcher, "Watchwords."

Jesus distinguished himself from his contemporaries and other supposed messiahs with his nonviolent, peacemaking approach to accomplishing great things on behalf of God's people, and the New Testament writers emphatically valued Jesus's position as "the Christ." Interestingly, Jesus never self-identifies as the Christ, or the Messiah. Confessions of this truth are always made by others, but Jesus *does* interpret these confessions, and he never denies them. For example, in Matthew 16 Jesus asks his disciples who they say he is, and Peter responds, "You are the Messiah [Christ], the Son of the living God" (v. 16). This is a dramatic confession, and Jesus has an answer to match it: "Blessed are you, Simon son of Jonah! For flesh and blood has not revealed this to you, but my Father in heaven" (v. 17). Jesus goes on to say that he will build his church on the rock of Peter and his good confession.

If the name Christ refers primarily to Jesus's human vocation, Logos turns our attention toward his divine nature. This is the great name of the Christ-hymn in the first chapter of John's Gospel, but it is also the name for Jesus in Revelation 19:13 ("He is clothed in a robe dipped in blood, and his name is called The Word of God"). Jesus is the Logos of God, the Word who exists in the thought of God before he is uttered in speech.

Logos is a clear indication of Christ's divine nature; "Son" has a more varied usage in Scripture, although after the third century it becomes the dominant name for Jesus among Christians. In the New Testament Jesus is the Son of Man, which, unlike Christ/Messiah, is how he refers to himself, with considerable frequency. Son of Man signifies a representative of the coming kingdom and the saints of the Most High, but the title is also an intensification of the term human being. Son of God was originally applied to angelic creatures (see Gen 6), but it came to herald a matter not of angelology or biology but of the election and mission of Israel. In Jesus's case, however, the name resonates deeply with names associated with his divinity, like Logos and another Son name, Son of the Father. Jesus refers to his Father as both "God" and "the one who sent me"; he instructs his disciples to pray to "our Father"; and he promises the coming of the Holy Spirit, who, according to the Apostle Paul, seals our adoption as children of the Father (see Rom 8:15; Gal 4:6).

Paul, or at least someone writing in his name, is the source for our fourth watchword name, Image. In Colossians 1:15, Christ "is the image of the invisible God." Prohibition of the worship of images as gods is bracing in the Old Testament and never denied by the New Testament writers, but the name Image carries with it the claim that God has provided for us what God has disallowed us from making. From the divine side, Christ is the uncreated Image, the Image not made by human hands; indeed, the Image not made at all: the eternal Image. For Christians, this means our images, or ideas, of God must conform to the Image of God who is Jesus Christ. From the human side, on the other hand, Jesus as Image is the Second Adam, the one faithful to the human vocation of Genesis 1, when God creates humanity "in our image, according to our likeness" (v. 26). All reflection on the image of God must be defined and normed christologically according to the true Image.

What about the name God? Several New Testament texts directly attribute the name to Jesus (John 1:1; John 20:28; Heb 1:8–9), or strongly suggest the connection (John 1:18; Rom 9:5; Titus 2:13; 2 Pet 1:1). And Jesus acts with Godly authority, with power at creation, as in Colossians 1, and sovereignty over creation through acts like the calming of the seas, walking on water, and the raising of Lazarus. Jesus plays a role in personal judgment, forgiving sins (Mark 2:5), and cosmic judgment (Matt 25:31). With Thomas, when we look to the Image we must declare, "My Lord and my God!" (John 21:28).

"My Lord": this final name forms the substance of the earliest Christian confessions and hymns about Jesus. If Messiah was probably the disciples' primary confession of faith during the earthly life of Jesus, Lord was certainly their chief affirmation of faith following the resurrection. We must remember that the English word "lord" is a translation of the Greek word *kurios*, which the Greek Old Testament (the Septuagint, or LXX) used to translate the Hebrew *Adonai*, the circumlocution for the divine name revealed to Moses on Mount Horeb (Exod 3:13–15). In other words, when we sing, "he is Lord, he is Lord, he is risen from the dead and he is Lord," we are saying that the son of Mary, the nephew of Elizabeth, the carpenter's son from Nazareth, is the God of Abraham, Isaac, and Jacob.

Conclusion

Jesus's nativity concerns much more than the birth of a baby, even of a baby who is our Savior. The nativity is the initial flowering of God's tree of life and of salvation in our midst. It is beautiful to behold, solemn to contemplate, and joyful to ponder. The Wesleyan tradition pauses at great length over this marvel, to consider the birth, the early life of Christ, and the names of Jesus. The tradition therefore challenges many of the cultural practices often associated with Christmas, not only those of secular society but also, even more so, those that can grip our churches in sentimentalism and ill-considered theology. Those of us who are inheritors of this Wesleyan tradition would do well to continue in it.

Questions for Consideration

1. How does the nativity of Jesus Christ heighten the scandalous nature of the incarnation?

2. What does the circumcision of Christ tell us about the mystery of the Word made flesh?

3. What may the circumcision of Christ tell us of the need of all Christians to grow in the love of God?

4. Why are the names of Jesus so significant to the person and work of Jesus?

5. What may the names of Christ communicate about the nature of God's salvation?

four

Baptism, Fasting, and Temptation

Lord, who throughout these forty days
for us didst fast and pray,
teach us with thee to mourn our sins
and close by thee to stay.

As thou with Satan didst contend,
and didst the victory win,
O give us strength in thee to fight,
in thee to conquer sin.

As thou didst hunger bear, and thirst,
so teach us, gracious Lord,
to die to self, and chiefly live
by thy most holy word.

And through these days of penitence,
and through thy passiontide,
yea, evermore in life and death,
Jesus, with us abide.

Abide with us, that so, this life
of suffering over past,

an Easter of unending joy
we may attain at last.[1]

This nineteenth-century hymn is one of only a few that deals directly with Jesus's post-baptismal fasting and temptation; it helpfully connects the Christian observance of Lent directly with Jesus's own forty days in the wilderness. The text, however, also reflects some curious decisions on the part of its author. First, there is no mention of Christ's baptism in the Jordan, even though the Synoptic Gospels agree that the baptism immediately precedes the fasting and the temptation. Of course, an artificial separation of these events is reinforced by a similar feature of the Western liturgical calendar, wherein the celebration of Christ's baptism falls on the Sunday after Epiphany, in early January, and the beginning of Lent is weeks later, in February or even March. Second, to return to the hymn text, the order of the stanzas does not reflect the New Testament chronology. In the hymn Jesus contends with Satan in the second stanza and fasts in the third stanza; in Scripture, on the other hand, Satan appears to tempt Christ only after Jesus has fasted at length.

The scriptural unity and order of these three events matters. The fasting, temptation, and even the public ministry of Jesus that follows are all manifestations of Christ's baptismal identity and vocation. In this chapter we examine the saving significance of Christ's baptism, fasting, temptation, and public ministry.

Baptism

In Matthew (ch. 3), Mark (ch. 1), and Luke (ch. 3), Jesus's baptism is the first reported event of his adult life and marks the beginning of his public ministry. As discussed in the previous chapter, we have surprisingly little scriptural information about Jesus's life after the nativity, and we have virtually no knowledge of his life between his journey to the temple (Luke 2) and his baptism. The Gospels tell us, however, that Jesus is no longer a boy or even a young adult by the time he is submerged in the Jordan River by John the Baptist; Luke says that he was thirty (Luke 3:23). Commenting on Christ's age, John Wesley suggests, "When he was of due

1. Hernaman, "Lord, Who Throughout These Forty Days," *United Methodist Hymnal*, No. 269.

age for executing his priestly office, he was manifested to Israel."[2] Thus Wesley connects the public manifestation of Christ's identity that occurs at the Jordan with Christ's vocation as the royal priest who accomplishes God's new covenant with his people.

The baptism itself is a Trinitarian event. While the Holy Spirit descends upon Jesus in the form of a dove, the Father's voice is heard from heaven: in Matthew, the Father declares, "This is my Son, the Beloved, with whom I am well pleased" (3:17); in both Mark (1:11) and Luke (3:22), "You are my Son, the Beloved; with you I am well pleased." In all three Gospels the declaration does not imply a "becoming," as if the Father were saying to Jesus, "Today you have *become* my Son." Rather, the language indicates a revelation of what is, what has been, and what always will be: this man Jesus is God's Son.

We must not allow the Trinitarian significance of this event to overwhelm its resonance with texts from the Old Testament. There is a very deep connection with the words of Psalm 2:7, "You are my son; today I have begotten you," which are spoken by the Lord in the midst of a royal psalm concerning the place of pride of the king of Israel. Christ now shares in this royal identity—indeed, he is "great David's greater Son."[3] At the same time, Isaiah 42:1 conditions the tone of this royal announcement: "Here is my servant, whom I uphold, my chosen, in whom my soul delights; I have put my spirit upon him; he will bring forth justice to the nations." Just as this verse from Isaiah comes at the beginning of the Song of the Suffering Servant, so, too, does its fulfillment in Christ's baptism augur a life of service through suffering.

Christ did not come to the Jordan to be washed of his sins; he who knew no sin needed no washing. His baptism was to reveal his identity to the world. Still, Christian baptism is modeled on Christ's. We become by grace what Christ is by nature: beloved children of the Triune God, royal priests with a calling to serve our Lord in a fallen and still unjust world. John Wesley says,

> Let our Lord's submitting to baptism teach us a holy exactness in the observance of those institutions which owe their obligation merely to a divine command. Surely thus it becometh all his followers to fulfill all righteousness.

2. J. Wesley, "End of Christ's Coming," 2.5.

3. Montgomery, "Hail to the Lord's Anointed," *United Methodist Hymnal*, No. 203, stanza 1.

Jesus had no sin to wash away. And yet he was baptized. And God owned his ordinance, so as to make it the season of pouring forth the Holy Spirit upon him. And where can we expect this sacred effusion but in an humble attendance on divine appointments?[4]

Fasting

The Gospels tell us that immediately after his baptism Jesus went into the wilderness for a forty-day retreat. Mark tells us, dramatically, that "the Spirit drove him out into the wilderness" (1:12). Matthew and Luke inform readers that Jesus fasted before he was tempted. Because more attention is devoted in those Gospels to the temptations, there is a tendency to overlook the fact that Jesus fasted first, but it is significant that he embraced this core spiritual discipline.

In his hymn on the saving mysteries of Christ, Charles Wesley devotes an entire stanza to Jesus's fasting:

By thy fasting and temptation
    Mortify our vain desires,
Take away what sense or passion,
    Appetite or flesh requires:
Arm us with thy self-denial,
    Every tempted soul defend;
Save us in the fiery trial,
    Make us faithful to the end.[5]

Fasting may be perceived as a kind of weakening of the body, but Wesley sees it more properly as a strength-building exercise. Fasting deadens "vain desires" and cuts away the pull of those desires, which takes us away from God, but in so doing fasting also empowers a person with weapons needed to withstand temptation and with the fortitude to endure times of trial.

Christ's act of fasting, therefore, was his final preparation for enduring the temptations of Satan. Whatever had preceded in his life surely had been used by God to ready him for his public ministry and for his

4. J. Wesley, *Explanatory Notes*, Matthew 3:16, 11.

5. C. Wesley, "Jesu, Show Us Thy Salvation," *Resurrection Hymns* (1746), Hymn 7, stanza 3.

proclamation of the coming of the kingdom of God. The baptism is the inaugural revelation of who Christ is; fasting is the embrace of the disciplined life required to be faithful to that revelation.

It is interesting that, in Wesley's hymn, Christ fasts vicariously for us. *Christ's* fasting, which in the hymn does not preclude *our* fasting, provides the source of strength *we* need to withstand temptation. Again, the whole of Christ's life is "for us and for our salvation." Not merely the instruction and the demonstrations of Christ's divinity that precede his atoning crucifixion and resurrection, but the acts of Christ themselves, have lasting significance for us. The gospel is not first and foremost a message *about* Jesus of Nazareth. The gospel *is* Jesus Christ.

Temptation

As we have just argued, the forty days of fasting in the wilderness built up Christ's spiritual fortitude, a necessary part of his divine-human existence. John Wesley says that "[by fasting] doubtless he received more abundant spiritual strength from God . . . As did Moses, the giver of the law, and Elijah, the great restorer of it."[6] But Satan believed that fasting had weakened Jesus and provided the opportune moment to tempt him away from his vocation. Matthew and Luke both say that Christ "was famished" after forty days in the wilderness.

The significance of the temptation lies in two related elements of the story: first, the very fact that Christ was tempted; and, second, the content of the temptations Satan believes might be effective against him.

Why was Christ tempted? Did Satan direct the temptations toward Christ's divine nature or his human nature? For that matter, was Christ *truly* tempted by Satan's propositions? To begin with, it must be said again that Satan, not God, is the source of the temptations. The Spirit drives Christ into the wilderness to prepare him for this trial, not to tempt him. In the Epistle of James the writer insists, "No one, when tempted, should say, 'I am being tempted by God'; for God cannot be tempted by evil and he himself tempts no one" (1:13). From this we must also answer that Satan's temptations clearly were directed at Christ's human nature and not his divinity. Still, the question of whether Jesus truly was tempted by Satan's words remains.

---

6. J. Wesley, *Explanatory Notes*, Matthew 4:2, 11.

A strict adherence to Christ's sinless nature might lead us to believe that the temptations were meaningless to him. But this strikes us as shading toward Docetism, the belief that Christ only appears to be human. Saying that the temptations were real to Christ does not at all take away from his sinlessness, because the sin is in the response. Moreover, insisting upon the reality of Christ's temptation strengthens his position as the one who has truly overcome human sin and weakness. This is the case made by the writer of Hebrews, who says that in Christ "we do not have a high priest who is unable to sympathize with our weaknesses, but we have one who in every respect has been tested as we are, yet without sin" (4:15). Jesus is tempted externally by the devil, but Satan's temptations strike at the heart of Jesus's internal desires.

Second, therefore, we should consider the content of the temptations themselves. Matthew and Luke agree on the content but differ on the order of the three temptations: the power to turn stones into bread, the opportunity to rule the kingdoms of the earth in exchange for worshiping Satan, and the challenge to prove God's providential care for him by jumping from the top of the Jerusalem temple. In each temptation, Satan deploys Scripture against Jesus, and Jesus rebuts Satan with Scripture. Taken as a whole, the temptations provide a perverse foreshadowing of events that will take place in Christ's public ministry: turning stones into bread anticipates his feeding of the five thousand; the kingdoms of the earth are fulfilled in the proclamation of the kingdom of God; and God's providence for Christ is proved when Christ is raised from the dead after his crucifixion.

There is also a certain irony in the temptations. Satan offers bread to the Bread of Life, seeks to be worshiped by the one who will draw all peoples to himself, and tries to insinuate doubt about God's faithfulness into the hypostatic union, the most intimate of all God-human relationships. In so tempting Christ, Satan comes across as a pathetic figure—not some fierce archrival to the divine plan but an unaware pretender.

Satan's miserable estate is reinforced by Christ's victory over him during the trial of temptations. By resisting Satan's temptations, Christ overcomes him and clears the final obstacle to the proclamation of the kingdom of God that will become the hallmark of the rest of his public ministry. After the temptations, Christ receives the ministrations of angels, which John Wesley suggests served two purposes: "Both to supply him with food, and to congratulate his victory."[7]

Public Ministry

Having laid claim to his baptismal identity and having overcome Satan, at least until "an opportune time" (Luke 4:13), Jesus enters fully into his public ministry. From now on, throughout the Gospels, he is a public figure, someone who is known and recognized by others as bearing authority. In this ministry, Christ himself is the *autobasileia*: Christ simply is the kingdom of God. Wherever he goes, there is the kingdom. By his presence, words, and deeds, he simultaneously proclaims and embodies God's reign.

The inaugural sermon, though found only in Luke 4, lays out the key markers of this ministry. Preached at Nazareth following his return from the wilderness temptation, the sermon consists of three parts: reading from the Isaiah scroll, a declaration of the fulfillment of that reading *today*, and a discourse about the rejection of Israel's prophets by those who should welcome them. John Wesley notes the Trinitarian significance of this passage,[8] in which, once again, the Spirit falls upon Christ the Son, who is set apart for a ministry to the poor, the captives, the blind, and the oppressed. All of this is centered around Jesus himself; it is a personal, not merely aspirational, proclamation.

There are significant moments within Christ's public ministry when this *autobasileia* is inescapable. John reports that Jesus's first miracle was to turn water into wine at a wedding feast in Cana, a sign of Christ's glory and a token of the messianic abundance of his life. Other miracles and deeds of power followed. He healed the sick and cast out demons, events that the Gospel writers often linked both thematically and chronologically. Sin and disease are not linked causally, but they are connected both by source (the work of Satan) and by cure (the more powerful work of Christ). In healing the sick, casting out demons, and forgiving sins Jesus breaks the power of Satan, over whom he has already demonstrated his eminent superiority.

Jesus also demonstrated remarkable authority over natural events, whether in the calming of the storm on the Sea of Galilee, or in the raising

7. J. Wesley, *Explanatory Notes*, Matthew 4:11, 11.

8. J. Wesley, *Explanatory Notes*, Luke 4:18, 89.

from the dead of a little girl or of his friend Lazarus. These events suggest that all of creation, and not just particular elements of human existence, is both out of sync with God's good intentions and still subject to God's royal power. Jesus enacts the full breadth of God's reign, which extends over all that God has made.

But perhaps one of the most remarkable features of Christ's ministry coincides with food and meals. As part of his kingdom proclamation, Jesus feeds large crowds miraculously. He takes a few loaves and fishes, only enough for a family, and provides for thousands. At the same time, he also shares table fellowship with sinners, to the dismay of the Pharisees. He tells them he has come to call sinners to repentance, but his presence suggests that sharing a table with sinners is part of how that call happens in the first place.

Matching his powerful deeds were Jesus's equally powerful words. Audiences remarked that "he taught them as one having authority" (Matt 7:29), and the inaugural sermon in Luke 4 ties that authority to the anointing of the Holy Spirit, rather than to some rhetorical prowess Jesus might have possessed. Jesus taught them concerning the law of Moses, which he both affirmed and radicalized. "Do not think that I have come to abolish the law or the prophets," he says at one point. "I have come not to abolish but to fulfill." In his teaching, as with his life, we discover that "fulfillment" means far more than ticking boxes on a checklist. He expands, concentrates, illuminates, and overflows what has come before so that what he teaches is both familiar and yet completely new.

At the heart of Jesus's teaching lies the Sermon on the Mount, the great sermon. Indeed, the Great Commission in Matthew 28 presupposes the great sermon in Matthew 5–7. Wesley preached extensively on the Sermon on the Mount and said this about its centrality:

> Knowing that happiness is our common aim, and that an innate instinct continually urges us to the pursuit of it, he in the kindest manner applies to that instinct, and directs it to its proper object.
>
> Though all men desire, yet few attain, happiness, because they seek it where it is not to be found. Our Lord therefore begins his divine institution, which is the complete art of happiness, by laying down before all that have ears to hear, the true, and only true, method of acquiring it.[9]

---

9. J. Wesley, *Explanatory Notes*, Matthew 5:2, 12.

The Beatitudes, the "you have heard it said, but I say . . ." sayings, and the teaching on prayer, forgiveness, and church discipline: here, Wesley says, is where we should look for happiness. Here, in other words, is the good news to the poor Jesus is sent to preach.

Conclusion

In his teaching and his life, Jesus's public ministry is a unified proclamation of the reign of God and the beginning of the fulfillment of his baptismal vocation. Overcoming Satan in the wilderness clears Christ's way to announce the kingdom of God powerfully by word and by deed.

Before arriving in Jerusalem, the culminating moment of this public proclamation is the Transfiguration, when Christ summits a mountaintop with Peter, James, and John and is changed, or transfigured, before their sight. There, on that mountaintop, he is seen for who he is, as divine glory shines through his flesh and his clothes. As at his baptism, a heavenly voice once again claims Jesus as God's Son, this time with a command—listen to him! These two manifestations of the Trinity, the baptism and the Transfiguration, display what is always true. Christ is God's Son; the Father, Son, and Holy Spirit are always present to him; and thus he is the *autobasileia*, the kingdom-itself-in-person. To seek first the kingdom of God is to seek Christ, his glory and his righteousness.

On that mountaintop Moses and Elijah appear together with Jesus and speak with him, discussing the coming new exodus Jesus would accomplish in Jerusalem (Luke 9:31). In this, too, the Transfiguration is a seminal event in Jesus's public ministry. For his teaching and his deeds of power all point to Jerusalem, where his public proclamation will become Christ's public humiliation, passion, and death.

Questions for Consideration

1. Why is the order of Christ's fasting, temptation, and baptism so important to grasping the significance of Christ's person and work?

2. How are John Wesley's insights into the public nature of Jesus's baptism helpful to understanding the Christian life as life under Divine Appointment?

3. How may we understand Christ's act of fasting as preparation for the enduring temptation of Satan? What is the connection between

fasting as a discipline and succumbing to temptation as a way of not fulfilling our vocation?

4. How do the temptations of Satan in the Gospels of Matthew and Luke strike at the heart of Jesus's internal desires, his mission?

5. How is Jesus's overcoming of temptation a sign of his manifesting the power of the kingdom of God, a living out of his baptismal identity?

6. How may Wesleyans, and Christians more generally, in both word and deed, enact or carry out the very power of God's mystery in Christ, God's *autobasileia*? What ministries may Christians themselves engage in to manifest such power?

five

Agony and Bloody Sweat

When Jesus wept, the falling tear
in mercy flowed beyond all bound.
When Jesus groaned, a trembling fear
seized all the guilty world around.[1]

This simple American folk hymn, just a single stanza, draws our attention toward an aspect of Christ's life we often overlook: his suffering. Among the saving mysteries of Christ are counted his agony and bloody sweat. Although the hymn does not mention either of these directly, like the saving mysteries it captures elements of Christ's suffering in Gethsemane. And that is important. Understandably, talk of suffering and Christ is also, usually, talk of the cross. The cross is where Christ suffers most, unto death. That is not, however, where Christ's agony, or struggle, and suffering begin. The tears, the groans, and the bloody sweat all precede the cross; they even precede the torture he endures at the hands of the Romans.

1. Morton, "When Jesus Wept," *Glory to God*, No. 194.

In the last chapter we discussed Christ's public ministry as a series of events inaugurating (as New Testament scholar N. T. Wright would say) the reign of God. That same ministry could also be characterized as a struggle, an agony, with some aspects even open to interpretation as a form of suffering. We will, in this chapter, therefore reconsider Christ's public ministry in light of that agony and suffering. Then we will turn, first, to the agony of Holy Week, before focusing on Gethsemane itself.

Some may wonder why we should bother dwelling on this subject at all, rather than simply noting it in passing. First, Joanna Cruickshank has demonstrated that suffering was a major theme in the hymns of Charles Wesley, which "are full of references to Christ's sufferings."[2] This emphasis divided John and Charles Wesley, but acknowledging Christ's suffering does mean acknowledging a major component of the Wesleyan heritage. Second, in his struggle and suffering before death, Christ exhibits his solidarity with suffering individuals and peoples of all ages. For Christ, as for so many, these are features of daily life, and not just a prelude to a tragic death. Third, recognizing Jesus's ongoing agony intensifies our contemplation of the saving mysteries of Christ. Truly Christ has emptied himself for us and for our salvation.

The Agony of Public Ministry

While it is true that Christ overcomes Satan in the wilderness and powerfully demonstrates his superiority whenever he heals the sick or casts out demons, at no point do the Gospels present his public ministry as a victory lap.

Once again, the inaugural sermon in Luke 4 is an excellent starting point. Jesus is filled with the Spirit. He preaches a word that excites his hometown synagogue. But when he mentions Elijah and Elisha, the crowd rejects Jesus, and the people try to kill him by throwing him off a cliff (vv. 28–30). To be sure, this event foreshadows Jesus's crucifixion, but it also presages the many rejections Christ will endure. In Mark 6:3–5, denizens of Jesus's hometown "took offense at him," and "he could do no deed of power there, except that he laid his hands on a few sick people and cured them." Matthew reports a similar problem in chapter 13. In John 1:46, one of the first disciples, Nathanael, expresses incredulity at the thought of a local savior: "Can anything good come out of Nazareth?"

---

2. Cruickshank, *Pain, Passion and Faith*, 48.

In each case, the people who might know Jesus best question, reject, or seek to harm him in the midst of the work and teaching of his public ministry. Mark further emphasizes this very personal rejection when he reports that members of Christ's own family tried to hold him back and declared him insane (3:21).

Beyond those who lived with and knew Jesus before his public ministry, many others who should have been sympathetic often expressed disbelief or rejected him outright. Recent scholarship has demonstrated that the Pharisees were Jesus's closest kin politically and theologically, but his controversies with them provide some of the most famous encounters in the Gospel narratives. Jesus's own disciples often demonstrated a remarkable inability to comprehend their master, whether in failing to understand his parables, or in seeking advantage for themselves in the kingdom of God, or in refusing to listen to his predictions of his betrayal and death. When Peter confesses that Jesus is the Christ, the Messiah, his beautiful recognition is quickly marred: as Jesus begins to speak of crucifixion, Peter tries to silence him.

Then there is Israel. The Synoptic Gospels specify that Jesus concentrated his ministry efforts on "the lost sheep of the house of Israel" (Matt 10:6 and 15:24), the people of God's covenant faithfulness. But here too is frustration and pain for Christ. The Herodian family, officially the indigenous rulers of Christ's people, harass Christ's family throughout his life. One Herod chases after Jesus at his birth and slaughters a town of innocent children in a vain attempt to kill the one whom the magi come to visit. Another Herod pursues John the Baptist, Jesus's cousin, until eventually he executes John, who has gotten caught up in a disturbing drama of family intrigue. The Pharisees tell Jesus that this same Herod also wants to kill him.

Meanwhile, Jesus finds in his ministry that "the lost sheep of the house of Israel" do not always seem interested in receiving their Good Shepherd. Jesus rebukes a crowd that follows him after he feeds the five thousand, telling them, "You are looking for me, not because you saw signs, but because you ate your fill of the loaves" (John 6:26). And Jesus mourns over his people before heading to the temple city: "Jerusalem, Jerusalem, the city that kills the prophets and stones those who are sent to it! How often have I desired to gather your children as a hen gathers her brood under her wings, and you were not willing!" (Luke 13:34).

Thus we see that Jesus's public ministry has two sides: the joy, excitement, and wonder of the self-proclamation of the kingdom of God; and the frustration, struggle, and agony of being misunderstood and rejected. Seeing the breadth of his public ministry from this perspective allows us to enter Jerusalem with him for Holy Week, the week that leads from Palm Sunday to Good Friday. Holy Week, in light of the ongoing agony of his ministry, is not a sudden, tragic turn of events. Instead, it has roots in the difficulties, even the suffering, Jesus has already endured from the very beginning.

The Agony of Holy Week

Though Holy Week is hardly the start of Christ's agonies, there is an undeniable increase, day by day, in their intensity as the triumphal entry leads to the *Via Dolorosa* (Way of Suffering).

At the beginning of the week, on the first day, Jesus enters Jerusalem riding a donkey, or the colt of a donkey. Jesus enters the holy city victoriously (see Zech 9:9) but not as its conqueror. He has not vanquished Israel, nor does he seek to do so, even as he enters as Israel's king. Yet while the disciples and the gathered crowds shout their hosannas, Jesus's mind is elsewhere. In his teaching and his life Christ has declared the way of peace as the way of the kingdom of God, and he enters Jerusalem peacefully. Luke reports, "As he came near and saw the city, he wept over it, saying, 'If you, even you, had only recognized on this day the things that make for peace'" (19:41–42). There has been a colossal failure to recognize "the things that make for peace," the things of the kingdom of God. So even this triumphal entry does not escape the agony of Christ's ministry.

Following this entry, the Gospel accounts differ on the precise timeline of the next days of Holy Week. For simplicity, we will follow Mark's timeline. In Mark's version, Jesus leaves the city after his royal entry and returns the following day to enter the temple. The temple itself, Israel's holiest site, then becomes yet another point of struggle for Christ. It has been overrun by those who have highjacked the temple for personal and political gain. Driving the moneychangers and the merchants from the temple is, for Jesus, an act of symbolic judgment upon the temple system, but it is not a moment of catharsis. Rather than relieving the pressure of Holy Week, it escalates matters, and contemporary New Testament scholars generally agree that it is this act more than any other that leads directly to Christ's crucifixion.

Holy Week is heavy with dismal ironies: the peaceful king whose people do not know peace; the need of a holy place to be sanctified by symbolic cleansing; the cleansing of the holy place by the Holy One of Israel leading to the crucifixion of the Holy One. Holy Week is tense, and the tensile force increases with each passing day. Having cleared the temple, Jesus reenters it the following day and teaches there at length. It seems possible, based on the accounts in Matthew, Mark, and Luke, that Jesus even taught there over several days. How strange it must have been for him, and for those around him, to do so in the very place whose way of being he had condemned so severely. And the force of his teaching concerns the further doom of the temple, its very destruction, if the people of Israel do not repent of their ways and find refuge in the kingdom of God.

By Wednesday, the decision to seek Christ's execution has been made by temple leaders. That night, a woman anoints Jesus "with an alabaster jar of very costly ointment of nard" (Mark 14:3) while he rests in Bethany, his safe haven away from the stress of Jerusalem. An act of love, poured out on the one about to pour his life out in love. It is beautiful, it is haunting, and Christ's disciples nearly ruin the moment with their petty moralism: "This ointment could have been sold for more than three hundred denarii, and the money given to the poor" (Mark 14:5). Christ's body is being prepared for death, and his disciples cannot see what is going on.

We find, in Holy Week, the painful humiliation of Jesus Christ. But even this humiliation is not wasted. Charles Wesley captures the strangeness of this week of pain:

> By thy sorer sufferings save us,
> > Save us when conformed to thee,
> By thy miseries relieve us,
> > By thy painful agony;
> When beneath thy frown we languish,
> > When we feel thine anger's weight,
> Save us by thine unknown anguish,
> > Save us by thy bloody sweat.[3]

---

3. C. Wesley, "Jesu, Show Us Thy Salvation," *Resurrection Hymns* (1746), Hymn 7, stanza 4.

To hear of Christ's "bloody sweat" is to hear of Gethsemane, the garden of agony that precedes Christ's passion and death. As John says, "Having loved his own who were in the world, he loved them to the end" (13:1). Those who followed him, who did not understand him, even the one who betrayed him, Jesus welcomes to a Passover meal like none other. And after the meal, when the one who has betrayed him had left, they depart for Gethsemane to pray.

The Agony of Gethsemane

Observing the "heroic behavior" of Christ in Gethsemane, John Wesley notes that Jesus endures both an outward conflict (the tears, the sweat, the anguished prayers) and an inward conflict, in which Christ finds, as an answer to his prayers, relief from fear of the passion and death that awaits him. The scene finds Jesus "surrounded with sorrow on every side, breaking in upon him with such violence, as was ready to separate his soul from his body."[4] The agony of Gethsemane confronts us with the depths of the incarnation, a confrontation that does not abate with the crucifixion. Here we find Christ, both human and divine, enduring remarkable suffering, with torment and anguish accompanied by an expressed desire for another way. How are we to understand this awful combination?

We begin by considering the nature of Christ's suffering itself in that garden. There is, foremost, the suffering of being on a path that will lead to a painful death. There can be no doubt, at this point, that Jesus expects to be killed, to be crucified, in short order. He is not yet condemned, but his is the agony of a man who knows what is coming and, seemingly, cannot escape it. This suffering isolates Jesus; it cuts him off from his friends and family and from the entire world. He leads his disciples to Gethsemane, only to go off by himself to pray.

Isolated from his friends, the disciples, Jesus also discovers the agony of their inability to accompany him in his suffering. Their teacher, their Lord, their Messiah displays every sign of being in traumatic pain, but they lack the fortitude to care for him, or even to pray with him—in fact, they cannot manage to stay awake but fall asleep on their watch. Surely this only adds to his suffering, a grief at how far they have come with him and yet how very far they still have to go.

4. J. Wesley, *Explanatory Notes*, Mark 14:33, 77.

That grief is compounded by the betrayal at the hands of Judas Iscariot. Each of the Gospels signals that Christ knew Judas would betray him before going to Gethsemane. Nevertheless, Judas betrays him with a kiss, turning a token of love and friendship into an act of violence against the peaceable king. Judas arrives with a posse, or better, a veritable lynch mob, demonstrating just how little anyone understands who Jesus is or what the kingdom of God is really like. Among the remaining disciples, some prepare to fight the mob, so Jesus must intervene as a peacemaker once more between those who want to hurt him and those who would defend him. But even this defense is revealed as feeble and half-hearted when the disciples run away in fear, leaving behind their clothes and their loyalty. Gethsemane is the nadir of the public ministry of Jesus Christ.

The actions of Jesus himself throughout these torturous moments are compelling. On the one hand, the Gethsemane events affect him deeply. "And going a little farther," Mark writes, "he threw himself on the ground and prayed that, if it were possible, the hour might pass from him" (14:35). Matthew 26:39 adds, "My Father, if it is possible, let this cup pass from me." He does not kneel; he throws himself on the ground to ask for another way. There is no show of suffering here; this is real for Christ. On the other hand the Gospels depict Jesus as someone who has accepted and entered willingly into what is to come. In John 12:27, Jesus says, "Now my soul is troubled. And what should I say—'Father, save me from this hour'? No, it is for this reason that I have come to this hour." Later, when his disciples attempt to take up arms in his defense, Jesus asks, "Am I not to drink the cup that the Father has given me?" (John 18:11).

A single prayer reconciles these two sides of Jesus's actions: "Not my will but yours be done" (Luke 22:42). At the Council of Chalcedon, the church recognized in Jesus Christ two distinct natures, human and divine, "without confusing the two natures, without transmuting one nature into the other, without dividing them into two separate categories, without contrasting them according to area or function."[5] If there are two natures, the church later affirmed, there are also two wills: one human, one divine. Yet these two wills do not compete against each other, nor is the human will subjugated to the divine will. The human will of Jesus Christ is free: free to express Jesus's desire for another way, and also free to conform, without coercion, to the divine will. Maximus the Confessor,

5. The Definition of Chalcedon, in Leith, *Creeds of the Churches*, 36.

the most ardent defender of the two wills of Christ, asks, "Is it a matter of resistance or courage, of agreement or disagreement? Certainly no one of a right mind will dispute that it is a matter neither of contention nor cowardice but of perfect harmony and concurrence."[6] The two wills are in harmony. Christ endures the agony of Gethsemane and enters into his passion with unity of purpose and will; he freely gives himself for the work of salvation that is yet to be completed.

Conclusion

Can God suffer? Can God die? What of Christ's suffering in Gethsemane and on Good Friday can be predicated of God? These are questions of divine (im)passibility. Advocates for divine passibility (the idea that God feels and suffers) can appeal to certain Scripture passages. In Jonah 3:10 God changes his mind about the punishment he was to inflict on Nineveh. In Genesis 6:6, we read, "And the LORD was sorry that he had made humankind on the earth, and it grieved him to his heart." And in Jeremiah 31:20, God is pained by Israel: "Is Ephraim my dear son? Is he the child I delight in? As often as I speak against him, I still remember him. Therefore I am deeply moved for him; I will surely have mercy on him, says the LORD." The promise of passibility is a straightforward interpretation of these passages, a God who is more like us, and a God who is in solidarity with our own sufferings.

But divine passibility also has serious problems.[7] There are Scripture passages that affirm, quite strongly, the unchanging, unchangeable nature of God (e.g., Num 23:19; Mal 3:6; Jas 1:17). There is a risk of obscuring or losing the Chalcedonian Definition, as the mystery of human suffering is swallowed up in the abyss of divine pain, and the scandal of the cross is relativized by the scandal of alienation within the Trinity. Divine passibility seems to eliminate the distinction between creature and Creator: if creatures who sin cause God to suffer, does that not make God just another creature? We also believe that divine passibility entails a loss of hope: can no one, not even God, be free from the suffering of a fallen creation?

Divine impassibility, the belief that God is not subject to change, is also not without problems. Divine impassibility can distance God from

---

6. *Opusculum* 6, in Maximus, *Mystery of Jesus Christ*, 173.

7. On what follows, see Weinandy, "Does God Suffer?"

humanity, making God seem so unlike us as to be unrelatable. And divine impassibility must wrestle with the very Scriptures that make divine passibility promising. But the promise of divine impassibility is greater still and, we believe, decisive. Impassibility affirms the drama of salvation is not a tragedy but a divine comedy. Suffering does not have the final word. All will be well. Impassibility finds comfort in God who is being itself (Exod 3:14) and especially in the biblical affirmation that God is love (1 John 4:8). God's existence supersedes creaturely suffering; because God is love, God does not respond to our suffering in order to satisfy some divine need or lack. God loves us freely and so can enter into the drama of our salvation with total regard for us. Bernard of Clairvaux has rightly said, God is impassible, but God is not without compassion.[8]

God in Christ suffers impassibly. The mystery of Christ's agony and bloody sweat is that these sufferings are real, human, and genuine—and yet they do not change or alter God in any way. God shares in these sufferings as only God can: in solidarity with us, yet able to help us and to overcome the sufferings not only of Christ but of the whole world.

Questions for Consideration

1. What are the two sides of Jesus's public ministry? How are they related?

2. What other words might we use to describe Jesus's last week? *Agony* is one. What others come to mind?

3. How did Jesus experience agony and rejection even before arriving in Jerusalem?

4. How does Jesus's agony and affliction in the Garden of Gethsemane speak to the mystery of salvation, to the mystery of who Jesus is and what he is doing?

5. What are the strengths and weaknesses of the argument for God's passibility? For God's impassibility? What are the dangers? How does God in the mystery of Christ's agony and bloody sweat share in this mystery yet overcome the suffering, all the while remaining God?

---

8. Bernard, *On the Song of Songs*, Sermon 26.3.5, 2:63.

six

Cross and Passion

They crucified my Lord,
and he never said a mumbalin' word;
they crucified my Lord,
and he never said a mumbalin' word,
not a word, not a word, not a word.

He hung his head and died,
and he never said a mumbalin' word;
he hung his head and died,
and he never said a mumbalin' word,
not a word, not a word, not a word.[1]

T he text of this spiritual is not meant to be taken literally. Jesus, in
   fact, does have a few very important words to say as he is crucified.
Rather, the spiritual draws on a long tradition of seeing in Christ's death
the fulfillment of Israel's Scripture. The Scripture text hinted at by this
hymn is Isaiah 53:7 ("He was oppressed, and he was afflicted, yet he did

1. "He Never Said a Mumbalin' Word," *United Methodist Hymnal*, No. 291, stanzas
1 and 5.

not open his mouth; like a lamb that is led to the slaughter, and like a sheep that before its shearers is silent, so he did not open his mouth"), a text that also finds echoes at several key moments during the Gospel narratives of the trial and execution of Jesus. With Psalm 22, Isaiah 52–53 provides the script for the passion drama.

The fulfillment of Scripture by Christ's crucifixion, however, should not inoculate us against the scandal, the foolishness, of our proclamation: at the cross he is INRI, *Iesus Nazarenus Rex Iudaeorum*, Jesus of Nazareth, King of the Jews. In this chapter we will consider further this fulfillment of Scripture. We will also reflect on the cry of dereliction, the atonement, and the confession that Christ died *sub Pontio Pilato* (under Pontius Pilate) in response to the holy mystery of Christ's cross and passion.

The Fulfillment of Scripture

By his crucifixion Christ suffers death in accordance with the Scriptures of the Old Testament. In fact, Christ's death superfulfills them. He does not just bring them to completion; he breathes new life and new meaning into them, even as he breathes his last. Overlapping in his passion are the exodus from Egypt, Israel's wilderness wandering, the sacrificial cult, and Isaiah's Suffering Servant. Psalm 22's cry of despair and narrative arc, which we will discuss in the next section, is also significant.

The story of the exodus figures prominently in Holy Week. Jesus's Last Supper with his disciples, at least in the Synoptics, has some of the characteristics of a Passover meal. It is certainly a meal eaten on the eve of the annual Passover celebration. Before Holy Week, in Luke's account of the transfiguration, we learn that Jesus goes to Jerusalem to accomplish his "departure" or new exodus. But Jesus isn't simply a new Moses. He is, at the same time, Moses, the slaughtered paschal lamb, and, as in John's Gospel, the "Way" itself.

When the Israelites escape from Egypt, they find themselves wandering in the wilderness. They complain, and their complaint becomes sin. The Lord sends snakes into the encampment, but Moses intervenes by prayer, and the Lord provides a cure for the punishment: "'Make a poisonous serpent, and set it on a pole; and everyone who is bitten shall look at it and live.' So Moses made a serpent of bronze, and put it upon a pole; and whenever a serpent bit someone, that person would look at the serpent of bronze and live" (Num 21:8–9). In John 3, Jesus becomes the serpent lifted on the pole. Although John does not explicitly link this lifting up with the cross, the inference is clear. Jesus does for the whole world what the crafted snake does for the Israelite camp.

The wilderness journey from Egypt to the Promised Land is also the context for the establishment of Israel's sacrificial cult. A significant component of the sacrificial cult was the making of atonement, a task to be performed by Aaron or by priests of the Aaronic order (the Levites). Atonement included the sacrifice of certain animals and the use of their blood in purification rites for the tent of meeting, the traveling holy site of the Israelites:

> No one shall be in the tent of meeting from the time he [Aaron] enters to make atonement in the sanctuary until he comes out and has made atonement for himself and for his house and for all the assembly of Israel. Then he shall go out to the altar that is before the LORD and make atonement on its behalf, and shall take some of the blood of the bull and of the blood of the goat, and put it on each of the horns of the altar. (Lev 16:17–18)

The writer of Hebrews picks up on this Aaronic ritual and casts Christ as both the priest and the sacrificial animal that yields the blood, for "when Christ came as a high priest of the good things that have come . . . he entered once for all into the Holy Place, not with the blood of goats and calves, but with his own blood, thus obtaining eternal redemption" (9:11–12). Christ's act is not a superseding of the cultic ritual, as if the ritual lost its meaning because of him, but rather Christ fulfills that ritual by expanding both its scope (for the whole world) and its meaning (eternal redemption).

Charles Wesley captures this well in his *Scripture Hymns*:

> The blood of goats and bullocks slain
> Had power to purge the legal stain,
>   And outward holiness restore,
> Sprinkled from his impurity,
> The sinner stood absolv'd and free,
>   And separate from the clean no more.
> And shall not that atoning blood
> Of Christ, the everlasting God,
>   A purer holiness impart,
> Make the polluted conscience clean,
> And purge our inmost soul from sin,
>   And sanctify our sprinkled heart?

Himself a spotless sacrifice
To his great Father in the skies
   He offer'd up for all mankind,
Thro' the eternal Spirit's power,
That cleans'd from sin we never more
   May soil with guilt our spotless mind:
That we may serve the living God
(When Satan's works are all destroy'd)
   The merits of our Lord demand;
And we his merits shall receive,
The life of pure obedience live,
   And bright in all his image stand.[2]

Notice two things about this hymn. First, Wesley affirms the saving power of the sacrificial cult, which really "had power to purge the legal stain." That power is assumed in order for Christ's sacrifice to "sanctify our sprinkled heart." Second, in the hymn's second stanza, Wesley gives this sacrifice a Trinitarian reading: Christ's offering is "to his great Father" and "thro' the eternal Spirit's power."

Lastly, we come to Isaiah's Suffering Servant, which we have said provides the script for the passion drama. Consider the following excerpts from Isaiah 53: "He was despised and rejected . . . Surely he has borne our infirmities and carried our diseases; yet we accounted him stricken, struck down by God, and afflicted . . . Upon him was the punishment that made us whole . . . All we like sheep have gone astray; we have all turned to our own way, and the LORD has laid on him the iniquity of us all" (53:3–6). Like the Suffering Servant, Jesus is mocked and rejected as one "struck down by God." His disciples scatter "like sheep." The Good Shepherd is abandoned by his own flock.

The imperial judgment at Jesus's crucifixion is that he is the "King of the Jews." The message is clear: following such a king is dangerous foolishness. In willingly submitting to the fulfillment of Israel's Scriptures, however, Christ turns this foolishness on its head. The irony of the cross is not that Jesus thought himself king and the Romans proved him wrong; the true irony is that on the cross Jesus shows himself to be the king, and the world has failed to recognize him.

2. C. Wesley, *Scripture Hymns* (1762), vol. 2, 700.

The Atonement: Christ for All

By superfulfilling Israel's Scriptures, Christ shows himself king not only of Israel but of the whole world. Peruvian Indian chronicler Felipe Guamán Poma de Ayala, who penned a lengthy and detailed account of the Incan people in response to Spanish colonialism, writes, "[Jesus] sent the Holy Spirit to give his grace to the holy apostles, so that they would go throughout the world preaching his gospel. Thus it was that the holy apostle Saint Bartholomew got the fortunate task, departed for Callo, and through his holy miracles left the Holy Cross of Carabuco."³

What Guamán Poma suggests, Jesus himself confirms in John's Gospel, saying of his death, "And I, when I am lifted up from the earth, will draw all people to myself" (12:32). More precisely, John the Baptist recognizes in Jesus "the Lamb of God who takes away the sin of the world" (John 1:29). Christ dies for all, for the forgiveness of sins of the whole world, which is "in accordance with the scriptures" (1 Cor 15:3).

The word often employed to capture this death for the sins of the whole world is "atonement." Atonement, or at-one-ment, is the act of reconciliation Christ accomplishes between humanity and God. Over the centuries various attempts have been made to say what exactly this atonement is and how it is accomplished. Randy Maddox has placed these attempts into three categories.⁴

First, there are images or models of the atonement that emphasize liberation and healing from the powers of death, sin, and the demonic. These include the Ransom Model, in which slaves to sin are set free; the Victorious Conqueror Model, in which Christ defeats these powers; and the Vicarious Healer Model, in which Christ is by death set free from death for the sake of the world. Second, there are images or models of the atonement that emphasize remedying the guilt and shame of sin, and the resulting alienation. These include seeing Christ's death as a sacrifice of purification, as in the discussion of Hebrews above, and the suggestion that Christ provides satisfaction for the demands of God's honor or justice. Third are images or models that point to Christ's death as a dramatic, or objective, display of God's love, which then provokes in humanity a response of love for God.

John and Charles Wesley affirmed the death of Christ was for the whole world; that is at the heart of their preaching and hymns. The

3. Guamán Poma, *New Chronicle*, 40ff.
4. Maddox, *Responsible Grace*, 96–109.

Wesleys also did not pick one sole model of atonement as definitive for themselves or for Methodists. Instead, they wove together the partial insights of the various images and models of atonement, while appealing to the wondrous love of God as the overarching framework.

The Cry of Dereliction[5]

In Mark 15:34 we read, "At three o'clock Jesus cried out with a loud voice, 'Eloi, Eloi, lema sabachthani?' which means, 'My God, my God, why have you forsaken me?'" Jesus's cry from the cross, often called the cry of dereliction, is undoubtedly a moment of deep pathos in the passion drama. This cry quotes Psalm 22:1 and seems to invoke the entire psalm, which speaks of a person whose condition can only be described as at the brink of death but also concludes with a bold proclamation of hope in God.

This cry has been subject to various interpretations. For some, it is a straightforward sign of divine forsakenness, with New Testament passages such as 2 Corinthians 5:21 and Galatians 3:13 seeming to support such a reading. Twentieth-century Swiss theologian Karl Barth famously argued, "Our sin is no longer our own. It is his sin, the sin of Jesus Christ."[6] Because on the cross Christ becomes our sin, the argument goes, God cannot associate with him any longer and forsakes him.

Another approach, different from but not necessarily incompatible with the first, is to see the cry as a prayer of faith and hope. One of the themes in British New Testament scholar N. T. Wright's work is that at the cross Jesus acts out the drama of Israel's abandonment and redemption in the exile and return from exile depicted in Old Testament texts. Psalm 22 likewise begins in prayer but ends in vindication. By offering a prayer from the cross drawing on that psalm, Jesus expresses hope, even prophetic hope, for his own vindication to come. Hope is not a matter of being cheerful in the face of difficult circumstances. Hope is a complex virtue in which expectation, desire, deprivation, and sadness can and often do go together. Also, a prayer of hope does not necessarily relieve suffering, even if that prayer is heard. In John's Gospel, after crying, "I thirst," Jesus is given wine on a sponge before dying. Similarly, in Luke's

---

5. We acknowledge the influence of Thomas J. White's article "Jesus' Cry on the Cross and His Beatific Vision" on what we write here.

6. Barth, *CD* 4/1:238.

account of Gethsemane, angels minister to Jesus, which strengthens him but also paves the way for even greater anguish.

A third possibility seems, to us, to incorporate strengths of these first two interpretations while also offering a point of departure for further fruitful theological reflection: the cry of dereliction as a cry of love. Christ's spiritual agony was an *effect* of his love for God and for humanity. He suffered because he loved, and by his suffering his love became manifest. Christ's intimacy with the Father intensified his sufferings, which were physical, emotional, and spiritual. His love for humanity was so intense that he even forsook "the experiences of consolation . . . which would normally be present even in the suffering of a virtuous man."[7] Christ's love for us is immeasurable, so the suffering caused by our sin that culminates in his crucifixion is likewise beyond all measure.

Charles Wesley seizes on the poetry of this dreadful moment: "'Tis mystery all: th' Immortal dies! / Who can explore his strange design? / In vain the firstborn seraph tries / to sound the depths of love divine."[8]

Sub Pontio Pilato

One of the striking features of both the Apostles' and Nicene creeds is that they include the names of only three people: Jesus, the Virgin Mary, and Pontius Pilate.[9] It is "under Pontius Pilate" that Jesus is crucified. Pilate names a historic and a political reality: Jesus died at a particular point in the past, at the hands of a particular imperial regime. But the inclusion of Pontius Pilate in the creed has not, unfortunately, stopped the church from finding a quite different target to blame for Jesus's death. In Matthew 27, Pilate symbolically washes his hands of Jesus's blood, to which the gathered crowd (or at least some in the gathered crowd) responds, "His blood be on us and on our children" (v. 25). Too many within the church have seen this response as an excuse to blame the Jews for the crucifixion, leading directly to the danger of anti-Semitism. It has proven all too short a road from Calvary to Auschwitz.

There is a better way. Let us consider the words prayed in Acts 4, after Peter and John are released by the Jerusalem authorities: "For in

7. White, "Jesus' Cry," 576.

8. C. Wesley, "And Can It Be," *Hymns and Sacred Poems* (1739), 118, stanza 2.

9. In the spirit of contemporary theologian Stanley Hauerwas, we might ask, "What the hell is an obscure first-century Roman governor doing in our creeds?!"

this city, in fact, both Herod and Pontius Pilate, with the Gentiles and the peoples of Israel, gathered together against your holy servant Jesus, whom you anointed, to do whatever your hand and your plan had predestined to take place" (vv. 27–28). First, this prayer is broadly inclusive: both Herod and Pontius Pilate, Rome and Israel, conspired or "gathered together" against Jesus. All of us are to blame. We would do well to heed the words of St. Francis of Assisi: demons did not crucify him; "it is you who have crucified him and crucify him still, when you delight in your vices and sins."[10] Anti-Semitism is ruled out; the Jews are not responsible for the crime of deicide because there are more actors on the stage.

Second, in this prayer the disciples say, "to do whatever your hand and your plan had predestined to take place." This echoes Galatians 4:4–5: "But when the fullness of time had come, God sent his Son, born of a woman, born under the law, in order to redeem those who were under the law, so that we might receive adoption as children." The cross is not a tragic accident or a big misunderstanding. The time, place, and cast of the crucifixion happened in accordance with God's saving will.

Third, Jesus suffered and died from love: obedient love to the Father and wounded love toward humanity. Speaking of God's will in relation to the cross means we must bear in mind the discussion of Christ's two wills from the previous chapter. In Jesus, the divine will is not opposed to the human, nor does the divine will superimpose itself on the human will. In the prayer from Acts, the word "predestined" is used, which can alarm Methodists. As with the two wills, however, predestination does not destroy Christ's freedom but instead enables it. Because what happens in Jerusalem is according to God's will and plan, Jesus is free to enter into his suffering also in accordance with the divine will.

Jesus speaks frankly of this freedom in John 10:17–18, saying, "For this reason the Father loves me, because I lay down my life in order to take it up again. No one takes it from me, but I lay it down of my own accord. I have power to lay it down, and I have power to take it up again." Christ freely submitted to the suffering inflicted upon him. In this way his death differs from ours. He had a choice, and he voluntarily accepted death. Indeed, since he is the author of life, some theologians consider his death to be the greatest of Christ's miracles. We consider it to be the greatest of his saving mysteries.

10. Francis of Assisi, *Admonitio* 5, 3, in *Catechism*, 170.

Conclusion

The events surrounding the cross, the passion, the death, the burial, the resurrection—these mark the highest point of divine disclosure. Yet the cross does not just concern Christ; the sign of the Cross is in the name of the Father, Son, and Holy Spirit. For it is at the cross that we see the mercy of God toward the world. At the cross, the Son surrenders the Spirit into the Father's hands. At the cross, the Father, out of love for the Son, bears him up and sustains him, even when the Son feels abandoned. At the cross, the Spirit is breathed out so that the witness of the water and the blood, the witness of the sacraments, may be true. The cross is the *Gnadenstuhl*, the mercy seat, from which the Triune Lord dispenses his love for his creation.

The Father is silent at the cross. No voice breaks through the clouds at Golgotha as once happened at the Jordan River. The Father is not silent because he is angry: how could he be angry? This is his beloved Son. Nor is the Father silent because he is indifferent: how could he who so loved the world suddenly become indifferent to it? The Father is silent because he is speechless. He has said it all in this one Word, and with the death of Jesus, the Father in a sense has been rendered mute. The final word from the cross is silence, the meaningful, merciful silence of the Father before the alleluias of Easter.

Questions for Consideration

1. How does the passion of Christ on the cross figure into the new exodus?

2. How are the hymns of Charles Wesley helpful in taking into account the mystery of God's love in Christ, into the very life of the Holy Trinity? What lines may stand out to speak of Christ's atoning work?

3. What is atonement? How did the Wesleys' understanding of the atonement of Christ for all distinguish them from other Christian groups, and what implications does such an understanding have for mission and ministry?

4. What are some of the possible meanings of Jesus's cry of dereliction on the cross?

5. What is the importance of Pontius Pilate to the mystery of salvation, and how may Christians today avoid the traps of anti-Semitism when dealing with the texts of Jesus's abandonment and crucifixion?

6. How may the mystery of the Holy Trinity serve to address the challenges of sin and the relationships between persons and groups?

seven

Resurrection and Ascension

Christ the Lord is risen today, Alleluia!
Earth and heaven in chorus say, Alleluia!
Raise your joys and triumphs high, Alleluia!
Sing, ye heavens, and earth reply, Alleluia!

Love's redeeming work is done, Alleluia!
Fought the fight, the battle won, Alleluia!
Death in vain forbids him rise, Alleluia!
Christ has opened paradise, Alleluia![1]

The resurrection of Jesus Christ is a cosmic event: it matters to all of creation; it is consequential for everything God has made. So Charles Wesley's "Christ the Lord Is Risen Today" exhorts "earth and heaven" to join in singing the Easter alleluia, recalling the creedal "seen and unseen" given life by the Creator. But it is also easy to pass over the "is" of the first line. Just as at Christmas we sing "Christ is born," not "Christ *was*

---

1. C. Wesley, "Christ the Lord Is Risen Today," *United Methodist Hymnal*, No. 302, stanzas 1 and 2.

born," so at Easter we sing "Christ is risen," not "Christ *was* risen."[2] The Easter resurrection, though an event in the historical past, reorients all of history around the risen Jesus Christ, so that the resurrection of Jesus is always present to us, no matter how far removed in time we may be from the historical event. The new creation begins with Christ's resurrection; "Love's redeeming work *is* done. Alleluia!"

Between Good Friday and Easter morning, however, there lies Holy Saturday. The mystery of Christ's passion and death yields to the mystery of Easter through the sepulchral repose of Holy Saturday.

Holy Saturday

The United Methodist Hymnal includes neither the phrase "he descended to the dead" nor "he descended to hell" in the Apostles' Creed, although the services of baptism contain the former. Nevertheless, this affirmation appears quite early in the history of the creed, with commentary on the descent appearing as early as the fifth century CE. John Wesley omitted the Church of England's Article III, "Of the going down of Christ into Hell," when he sent the revised Articles of Religion for the new Methodist Episcopal Church in the United States. And in the *Notes upon the New Testament*, Wesley dismisses the idea that Jesus actually went to hell.

The scriptural evidence itself is ambiguous. There are passages that talk about Christ's descent (Eph 4:9) or his preaching to those who have already died (1 Pet 3:19), but Wesley sees that these passages do not necessarily refer to an actual entrance into hell by Jesus. The descent in Ephesians could refer to Christ's incarnation, and as for 1 Peter 3:19, Wesley speculates that the dead were in a kind of prison rather than hell. What Wesley does not deny is the heart of this clause: that Jesus truly died, and that Jesus is truly victorious.

Many other theologians and preachers have insisted on the significance of the descent to the dead, indeed, the descent to hell. In patristic and scholastic accounts, the descent to hell marks the beginning of the resurrection. Thomas Aquinas provides an especially nuanced version of this position. For Aquinas, the descent into hell was for Christ to bear the full punishment for sin, to conquer the devil, to comfort his friends, the patriarchs, and to deliver the saints. Aquinas also understands hell to have

---

2. We owe this observation to a remark made by Nicholas Wolterstorff in a lecture at Duke Divinity School some years ago.

different parts, and for him Christ does not descend to the hell of the lost. (John Wesley might have found this way of saying things reassuring.)

In this earlier period of church history, writers also look to this descent as a reconstituting of hell and as a sign of the universal availability of salvation. In his descent, Christ is said to have harrowed hell, removing from its grasp the patriarchs and others who had died before Christ's own death. Thus hell is reconstituted from Christ's descent onward, as only those who refuse that salvation (the truly damned) remain. Also, by submitting to this descent, Christ makes salvation available to all, not just those who had the good fortune of living when he walked the earth or thereafter. Salvation is universally offered.

In the Reformation era, the emphasis shifts to seeing Christ's descent as the final act of his passion. In the Heidelberg Catechism, the question is asked, "Why is it added: He descended into Hades?" The response given is, "That in my greatest temptation I may be assured that Christ, my Lord, by his inexpressible anguish, pains, and terrors which he suffered in his soul on the cross and before, has redeemed me from the anguish and torment of hell."[3] Here the descent into hell completes the sufferings of Christ on the cross.

In Fyodor Dostoevsky's *The Idiot*, a Renaissance-era painting by Holbein of the dead Christ prompts Prince Mishkin to exclaim, "That picture! A man could lose his faith looking at that picture!"[4] The same may be said by many Methodists with respect to Holy Saturday, a shrouded mystery if ever there was one. Rowan Williams, however, counters that "it is precisely in contemplating Jesus's death that faith grows stronger and receives a dazzling light; then it is revealed as faith in Christ's steadfast love for us, a love capable of embracing death to bring us salvation . . . Christ's total self-gift overcomes every suspicion and enables me to entrust myself to him completely."[5] Holy Saturday deserves our greater contemplation. On the cross the Gospels record seven last words of Jesus; here is the eighth word, before the eighth day, the word of the Father's silence. Here, too, Christ lies in full solidarity with those who have died. Here, with Christ, we also pass from death to life, as Charles Wesley writes:

3. Cited in Jones, "John Calvin's Reception," 224.

4. Dostoevsky, *Idiot*, 227.

5. Williams, *Dostoevsky*, LF 16.

From the world of care release us,
By thy decent burial save,
Crucified with thee, O Jesus,
Hide us in thy quiet grave:
By thy power divinely glorious,
By thy resurrection's power
Raise us up, o'er sin victorious,
Raise us up to fall no more.[6]

The Resurrection

In 1 Corinthians 15 the Apostle Paul addresses the centrality, even the necessity, of the resurrection head on: "and if Christ has not been raised, then our proclamation has been in vain and your faith has been in vain" (v. 14). On the third day Christ rose from the dead, "and took again his body, with all things appertaining to the perfection of man's nature, wherewith he ascended into heaven, and there sitteth until he return to judge all men at the last day."[7] The resurrection is not a mere resuscitation. This is a unique happening, a new creation. The Risen One is risen in body, comes to his people victorious, and approaches them lovingly, without blame.

The church treasures several important signs of Christ's resurrection. There is, first of all, the empty tomb. Although the Gospels differ in how they describe the tomb's discovery, all agree that Christ's tomb was empty, and in all four Gospels that discovery is a shock to Jesus's followers. The Gospels also report several specific appearances of Jesus to his disciples. He appears to them on their way to the Upper Room (Matt 28:8–10); he walks with them on the way to Emmaus (Luke 24); he speaks with them in the garden (John 20:10–18); he enters the Upper Room where they have gathered (Luke 24:36–49; John 20:19–29); and he prepares breakfast for them by the Sea of Tiberius (John 21).

In addition to the empty tomb and the appearances, there are the witnesses to the resurrection: the women at the tomb, Mary, and the Eleven. Also, there are the sacraments, in which the living Jesus presents himself to his faithful from generation to generation.

6. C. Wesley, "Jesu, Show Us Thy Salvation," *Resurrection Hymns* (1746), Hymn 7, stanza 6.

7. The Articles of Religion of The United Methodist Church, Article III.

Jesus's resurrection does not mark his physical withdrawal from creation: far from it, in fact. There is a forty-day period between Christ's resurrection and his ascension. During this Easter season, Jesus participates in very ordinary activities: he eats, he advises on fishing, he walks, he sits. But these forty days are also a time of extraordinary encounters. Jesus's resurrected body does not seem subject to the same restraints and conditions as our unredeemed flesh. He comes and goes as he pleases. Sometimes he is recognized, and sometimes his disciples struggle to see him for who he is. His encounters with them provoke joy and sorrow, doubt and faith.

Not all of Jesus's appearances are recorded in detail in Scripture. As in the rest of his earthly life, there are hints of further activity that are no longer known by us. Paul mentions appearances "to more than five hundred brothers and sisters" as well as to James and to himself (1 Cor 15:3–8). Paul's list of appearances suggests that there might be further appearances unknown to him or to us. Did Jesus appear to his mother? Did he travel to other lands around the world? There is no biblical reason to answer no to either question.

What we do know of his appearances is that Jesus uses them to teach his disciples further. He instructs them concerning the Suffering Messiah, in whom humiliation and exaltation coincide salvifically. He teaches them that his work represents the fulfillment of Israel's Scriptures. And he gives this new community, formed around their resurrected Lord, its evangelical mission. The mission is Trinitarian, done "in the name of the Father and of the Son and of the Holy Spirit" (Matt 28:19); it is communal: Jesus instructs a plural "you" in the closing chapters of the Gospels. The mission is sacramental: baptism is its cornerstone in Matthew 28 and Mark 16. The mission is also one of reconciliation. In John's Gospel, Jesus blesses his disciples with "Peace" and then commissions them "as the Father has sent me" to forgive sins in the power of the Holy Spirit (20:21–23). In Luke 24, Jesus tells them "that repentance and forgiveness of sins is to be proclaimed in his name to all nations, beginning from Jerusalem" (v. 47). Thus the new community, the church, goes into the world as Jesus lived in the past and continues to live in the present.

The forty days after the resurrection also introduces a time of misidentification. The risen Christ has a real body (he can be touched; he can eat), but it is a strange body. He is not immediately recognizable, and he can walk through walls. These misidentifications are not just happenstance. "Misidentifying" Christ means that Christ's body can be recognized, truthfully, in the bodies of others. At the tomb, he is mistaken for the gardener, and he is the new Adam, the gardener of the new creation. On the road to Emmaus, he is taken for a stranger, or a foreigner, and his disciples are sent in his name to be sojourners, wayfarers, and strangers in the world. On the road to Damascus, Christ "misidentifies" himself to Saul, telling the future apostle, "I am Jesus, whom you are persecuting" by pursuing his followers in Jerusalem and beyond (Acts 9:5).

This "misidentification," then, persists beyond the forty days, even up until today. In the bread and wine of the Eucharist the church continues, rightly, to recognize, or "misidentify," the body and blood of the risen Christ. In Matthew 25:40 Jesus says that at the last judgment, "The king will answer [those who are judged], 'Truly I tell you, just as you did it to one of the least of these who are members of my family, you did it to me.'" By these words the church is commanded to recognize, to "misidentify," Jesus in the poor, the widow, the sick, the imprisoned, and the stranger: in whoever is the least in our world. After the resurrection we must sing:

> When the poor ones who have nothing share with strangers,
> when the thirsty water give unto us all,
> when the crippled in their weakness strengthen others,
> then we know that God still goes that road with us,
> then we know that God still goes that road with us.[8]

The Ascension

The Feast of the Ascension falls forty days after Easter, which is (always) a Thursday. For this reason, many in the Wesleyan tradition pass by the feast day without much notice, unless their particular congregations commemorate the day on the following Sunday. The ascension, while a different event, is integral to the logic of the resurrection. Christ who has descended to earth for us and for our salvation now ascends to heaven to be "seated at the right hand of the Father."

One of the major themes in John Wesley's occasional christology is the importance of preaching Christ in all his offices: "We are not ourselves clear before God, unless we proclaim Christ in all his offices."[9] In "A

8. Olivar and Manzano, "Cuando El Pobre (When the Poor Ones)," *United Methodist Hymnal*, No. 434, stanza 1.

9. J. Wesley, Sermon 36, I.6.

Letter to a Roman Catholic," Wesley summarizes his faith in Jesus Christ by referring to these offices:

> I believe that Jesus of Nazareth was the Savior of the world, the Messiah so long foretold; that, being anointed with the Holy Ghost, He was a Prophet, revealing to us the whole will of God; that He was a Priest who gave Himself a sacrifice for sin, and still makes intercession for transgressors; that He is a King, who has all power in heaven and in earth, and will reign till He has subdued all things to Himself.[10]

Prophet, Priest, and King: these are the offices of Christ.

As Prophet, Jesus teaches with authority in word and by deeds of power. He speaks through and enacts the words of the prophets of the Old Testament in order to fulfill them. He fulfills, renews, and reinscribes the law within the new covenant of grace, continuing to speak to the church. As Priest, Christ propitiates the wrath of God by his righteousness, which is fully divine and fully human. He is the Divine-Human mediator, interceding for us on the cross through his priestly sacrifice of himself and through his life of devout prayer, especially his prayer for the gift of the Holy Spirit. As King, Jesus Christ announces the reign of God, the kingdom of God, from the time of his baptism on. Wherever he goes, there is the kingdom of God, because he is its King. It is the kingdom of grace, sanctifying believers, gathering the church, and showing mercy at the last judgment, but it is also the kingdom of glory, the blessedness of the Christ's followers and the coming of the eternal heavenly city.

The ascension fulfills the three offices of Christ. The ascension is God's "yes" to the power exercised by the true David, the power of faith, hope, and love. Echoing Psalm 47, a royal psalm prescribed by lectionaries throughout the church's history for the Feast of the Ascension, Charles Wesley writes,

> God is gone up on high
> > With a triumphant noise,
> The clarions of the sky
> > Proclaim the angelic joys!
> Join all on earth, rejoice, and sing,
> > Glory ascribe to glory's King.[11]

10. J. Wesley, "Letter to a Catholic," in *Works* (Jackson), 10:80–86.

11. C. Wesley, "God Is Gone Up on High," *Ascension Hymns* (1746), Hymn 2, stanza 1.

The ascension is the coronation of the true David, the coronation of the King of the Jews as the King of the universe. Jesus is now at the right hand of God as the symbol of divine victory and power. In the Nicene Creed we profess that "His kingdom will have no end"—a clause intended as a rebuke to the belief that the Second and Third Persons of the Trinity were only temporary manifestations. Christ continues to reign even after his ascension to the Father, for his ascension is his coronation, the beginning of his eternal reign. And Christ is King of kings and Lord of lords, forever.

The ascension is also the consecration of the true Aaron. Again, we hear from Charles Wesley:

> Hail, Jesus, hail, our great high priest,
> Entered into thy glorious rest,
>   That holy happy place above!
> Thou hast the conquest more than gained,
> The everlasting bliss obtained
>   For all who trust thy dying love.[12]

Jesus is our high priest, "who in every respect has been tested as we are, yet without sin" (Heb 4:15). His first high priestly prayer upon his consecration is the Pentecostal *epiclesis*, the prayer for the Father to send out the Holy Spirit upon the disciples of Jesus Christ. Pentecost depends upon the ascension; the ascension leads to Pentecost. As high priest, Jesus Christ is uniquely our mediator and our intercessor. Yet he also institutes a new priesthood, a sharing in his ministry of mediation and intercession, a "royal priesthood" who offer themselves as "a living sacrifice, holy and acceptable to God," "in the priestly service of the gospel of God" (1 Pet 2:9; Rom 12:1; 15:16). And as there is no end to his reign, so his priestly intercessions are eternal.

Finally, the ascension marks the exaltation of the true Elijah, the prophet taken up to heaven in a whirlwind. Charles Wesley sees this, too, of Christ:

> All hail the true Elijah,
> The Lord our God and Saviour!
>   Who leaves behind,
>   For all mankind,
> The token of his favour.
> The never-dying prophet,
> Awhile to mortals given,

---

12. C. Wesley, "Hail, Jesus, Hail," *Ascension Hymns* (1746), Hymn 4, stanza 1.

> This solemn day
> Is rapt away
> By flaming steeds to heaven.[13]

In the New Testament, Elijah is identified as the prophet who was to come before the end of the world, and Elijah is associated with John the Baptist, the forerunner, the friend of the bridegroom. When Jesus asks his disciples, "Who do people say that I am?" the reports include both Elijah and prophet. Jesus spoke as a prophet, appears to have thought of himself as a prophet, and wrought miracles as prophets in Israel's past had done. He warns his disciples that he and they will face the persecution all of God's prophets must endure. But Jesus surpasses all other prophets, because he is both the message and the messenger. He does not speak of one to come, for he is the one who has come. Elijah, at his ascension, passes his mantle and a double portion of his spirit to Elisha, but Jesus, at his ascension, passes a nobler mantle to his followers, which is the Holy Spirit poured out upon them.

The ascension, then, is not about Jesus's "going away." He is enthroned in heaven, but he is also, and always, still here, for you, in the sacraments, in the church, and in the least of the world. The ascension celebrates the completion (but not the end) of Christ's offices: the Prophet, Priest, and King of God's salvation.

Conclusion

In his saving work for us, Christ passes from the repose of Holy Saturday through the glory of new life in the resurrection to exaltation to eternal rest upon his heavenly throne. In this, he is the pioneer of our own faith, hope, and love. We who submit, in baptism, to a death like his will also follow him from rest to resurrection to glorification. The promise of God's covenant in Christ is that the royal priesthood is established forever, not just for Christ but for all who follow him.

The seal of this promise is nothing less than God's very self, the gift of the Holy Spirit Christ gives to us in his final saving mystery.

---

13. C. Wesley, "All Hail the True Elijah," *Resurrection Hymns* (1746), Hymn 16, stanza 1.

Questions for Consideration

1. Why do many Christians avoid Holy Saturday? Are there Christian groups that still do not confess that Jesus "descended into hell"?

2. How does Jesus's death on the cross and time in the tomb speak to the power and presence of God's mystery of salvation on Easter?

3. What are some of the important signs of Christ's resurrection? Why are these signs significant to understanding the mystery of Christ? What do they tell us about the way the church is to minister in the world?

4. How may Christians, and Wesleyans in particular, bypass the ascension?

5. How is the ascension really integral to the logic of the resurrection? What does this say about who Christ is as the judge and ruler of all, as Prophet, Priest, and King?

6. How do the three offices of Christ speak to the mystery of Christ and to the way we are to carry out ministry—to the kinds of dispositions Christians are to demonstrate when working among the poor or excluded, for example?

eight

The Coming of the Holy Spirit

For your gift of God the Spirit,
power to make our lives anew,
pledge of life and hope of glory,
Savior, we would worship you.
Crowning gift of resurrection,
sent from your ascended throne;
fullness of the very Godhead,
come to make your life our own.[1]

The opening stanza of this beautiful hymn by Margaret Clarkson reminds us of a powerful truth: Pentecost is the last feast of the Easter season, and the coming of the Holy Spirit is the "crowning gift of resurrection." The Spirit does not come independently of the Son any more than the Son could have been incarnate bereft of the Spirit. And, in the order of salvation the Spirit is the gift of the Son, of Jesus Christ, to his followers in order, as the hymn says, "to make [Christ's] life our own." The

---

1. Clarkson, "For Your Gift of God the Spirit," stanza 1.

Spirit, as theologian Jürgen Moltmann has claimed, is the Spirit of life,[2] but we must be precise with our language: the Spirit is the Spirit of the life of Jesus Christ.

In this final reflection on the saving mysteries of Jesus Christ, therefore, we will consider the role of the Spirit in the fullness of these saving mysteries. We will then turn to Pentecost as the inauguration of an in-between epoch, an era of the middle advent. In sending the Spirit Jesus gives a down payment that augurs his second, and final, return to judge the living and the dead.

A Spirit Christology

The work of salvation God accomplishes in Jesus Christ is properly the subject of christology. Christology, however, is also and always a matter of Trinitarian theology more broadly. The Father, Son, and Holy Spirit are thoroughly caught up in who Jesus Christ is and what he does, even if we must also and always say that only the Second Person, only the Son, is incarnate "of the Holy Spirit and the Virgin Mary." One of the tools of theology to emphasize the Triune nature of christology is to speak of a Spirit christology, which draws attention to the role of the Spirit in the life of Jesus Christ.

We can begin, as it were, at the beginning, with the incarnation itself. In Luke 2, when Gabriel visits the Virgin Mary, he promises that the Holy Spirit will come upon her powerfully in order that she might bear a son, who will be Jesus. The Spirit makes possible the incarnation, so it is not a stretch to say that everything that happens in the life of Jesus happens because of the Spirit. Mary is hardly the first Israelite to receive the Spirit in a powerful way; the Old Testament has many stories of the Spirit coming upon individual prophets and leaders of the people of Israel. Mary, however, receives the Spirit so thoroughly that the prophetic word she speaks is the Word Made Flesh.

At Christ's baptism in the Jordan River, the heavens open, the Father speaks his love for his Son, and the Spirit descends as a dove. Following the baptism, the Spirit leads Jesus into the wilderness for forty days of fasting; as we noted in chapter 4, the Gospel of Mark gives strong agency to the Spirit here: "The Spirit drove him out into the wilderness" (1:12). The Spirit energizes Christ's preparation for and initial steps into his

---

2. Moltmann, *Spirit of Life.*

public ministry. Upon his return from the wilderness, Jesus preaches that he fulfills the Scripture text that "the Spirit of the Lord is upon me" (Luke 4:18).

At no point in the Gospels is there any suggestion that the Spirit is removed from Jesus. Everything Christ does, he does in the Spirit. He is the Spirit-Prophet who fulfills all prophecy; the Spirit-Priest who intercedes in prayer and teaches how to pray; and the Spirit-King who reigns in the kingdom of God, which is "righteousness and peace and joy in the Holy Spirit" (Rom 14:17). True, after the baptism and the inaugural sermon, direct references to the Holy Spirit recede (although they do not disappear). But there are important reminders along the way. In Luke 11, Jesus rebuts the accusation that he works in league with Beelzebul, telling his accusers, "But if it is by the finger of God that I cast out the demons, then the kingdom of God has come to you" (v. 20). Since the patristic era Christians have identified the Spirit with the phrase "finger of God." The Holy Spirit, the finger of God, is the sign that Christ has brought about the kingdom of God.

As we move into Holy Week, the enduring presence of the Holy Spirit in Christ's life becomes more and more important. The agony of Christ's life, whether the agony of his public ministry or the acute agony of the week following Palm Sunday, is borne by Christ in concert with the Holy Spirit. Christ's groans in Gethsemane reverberate with the groans of all creation that the Spirit offers to the Father in prayer (Rom 8). And the cry of dereliction—is it possible to imagine a better example of the "sighs too deep for words" the Spirit prays on our behalf (Rom 8:26)?

Truly Christ prays in the Spirit as he endures the passion and crucifixion. Perhaps it is no coincidence, then, that Christ's promises of the Holy Spirit come during these days of agony. The Final Discourse in John's Gospel (chs. 14–16) is full of Jesus's teaching concerning the coming of the Holy Spirit, another Comforter, who will bring to mind all that Jesus has taught the disciples as they have need.

On the Sabbath between Good Friday and Easter, the Son rests in the grave, the Father rests in a silent word, and the Spirit rests upon the Son. And as the Son harrows hell, he does so with the Holy Spirit, who is sent by the Father in tandem with the Son. The lectionary passages for Holy Saturday include excerpts from Lamentations 3. The reading begins, "I am one who has seen affliction under the rod of God's wrath," but the tone shifts near the reading's close: "The steadfast love of the LORD never ceases, his mercies never come to an end" (Lam 3:1, 22). Even in the tomb, the bond of love does not break. Even in the grave, the love the Father shares with the Son by the Holy Spirit endures.

But on Easter, yes on Easter, the Father raises the Son by the power of the Holy Spirit (Rom 8), the Spirit of life, the Spirit of the life of Christ. In the days following Easter, Jesus continues to exercise his offices of Prophet, Priest, and King as he opens the Spirit-breathed Scriptures to his followers, or as he breathes on them to receive the Spirit for the forgiveness of sins, or as he commands them to go forth and be his witnesses in the power of the Spirit. Finally, following his ascension, Jesus gives the gift of Pentecost, when the Spirit is poured out, not just on particular individuals, but on "all flesh" for the sake of the kingdom of God (Joel 2:28).

Pentecost

The giving of the Spirit follows upon the resurrection and the ascension, and it is the final sign of Christ's triumph before his second coming. At Pentecost, Christ *gives* the Holy Spirit, sealing his divinity; only God can give of God. At Pentecost, Christ sends the Spirit to give life, his life, to those who believe in his name and confess him as Lord. At Pentecost, Christ pours the Spirit out on the whole world; his kingdom is shed of all restraints.

In the liturgical calendar, Pentecost closes out the Easter season and opens into "ordinary time" or the season after Pentecost, which lasts until the following Advent. Ordinary time has integrity in its own right: it is a season for growth in discipleship and for attending to the teachings of Jesus. But it is also an in-between time, just as the epoch following the first Pentecost is an in-between time, a "now" of bearing witness to the gospel and a "not-yet" of waiting for the new creation. Charles Wesley writes,

> By the coming of thy Spirit
>   As a mighty rushing wind,
> Save us into all thy merit,
>   Into all thy sinless mind;
> Let the perfect gift be given,
>   Let thy will in us be seen,
> Done on earth as 'tis in heaven:
>   Lord, thy Spirit cries Amen![3]

3. C. Wesley, "Jesu, Show Us Thy Salvation," *Resurrection Hymns* (1746), Hymn 7, stanza 9.

"Let thy will in us be seen, / Done on earth as 'tis in heaven: / Lord, thy Spirit cries Amen!" Amen—not "it is finished," but "so let it be."

There are five major characteristics of this in-between time. First of all, it is a time of questions. In Acts 1:6, the disciples ask, "Lord, is this the time when you will restore the kingdom to Israel?" How long, Lord, must we wait? The "not-yet" of this era prompts such questions and drives Christ's followers back to the Scriptures and back to his teachings, seeking the wisdom to endure these questions with patience. For this reason, this time is, second, a time of groaning (Rom 8:24). Knowing what is to come and yet not knowing when it will arrive can be agonizing, as anyone in the midst of childbirth would testify. Adding to the struggle are the constant reminders that the kingdom has not arrived in its fullness: the shedding of blood, the oppression of the poor, the indifference to suffering.

Still, third, the season is a time of joy, also. At the end of Luke's Gospel, in the first account of the ascension, the disciples "returned to Jerusalem with great joy; and they were continually in the temple blessing God" (24:52–53). Similarly, after Pentecost the first believers "spent much time together in the temple . . . praising God and having the goodwill of all the people" (Acts 2:46–47). The book of Acts does not read as a slog through the muck of the world but as a testimony to the persistence of joyful obedience to Jesus Christ, even in the face of trials and persecutions.

Fourth, the in-between time is set aside for watchfulness. Jesus's warning, "Beware, keep alert; for you do not know when the time will come" (Mark 13:33), is meant as a constant reminder to all generations of his disciples. Attempts to historicize this claim, and others like it throughout the New Testament, by suggesting the first generations of his followers were caught up in overly optimistic expectations of his imminent return miss the point. Watchfulness is a hallmark of those who have received the Spirit; they watch because the very presence of the Spirit is the guarantee that God has a future that is still to come.

Finally, this epoch of questioning, groaning, joy, and watchfulness is a period of hope. Hope, we have said, is a complex virtue, so it is the comprehensive characteristic of this in-between time. As Paul says, "For in hope we were saved. Now hope that is seen is not hope. For who hopes for what is seen? But if we hope for what we do not see, we wait for it with patience" (Rom 8:24–25); further, "hope does not disappoint us, because God's love has been poured into our hearts through the Holy Spirit that has been given to us" (Rom 5:5).

This period of hope can also be described as a middle advent. Medieval theologian Bernard of Clairvaux explains:

> We have come to know a threefold coming of the Lord. The third coming takes place between the other two . . . his first coming was in the flesh and in weakness, this intermediary coming is in the Spirit and in power, the last coming will be in glory and majesty.[4]

Far from being Christ's removal from us, Pentecost is Christ's advent to us, different in kind from the advent of the incarnation or the advent of the second coming, but nevertheless an advent, a coming to us. The middle advent is a Trinitarian event; in John 14:23 Jesus says, "Those who love me will keep my word, and my Father will love them, and we will come to them and make our home with them." The Father loves those who keep Christ's word through the gift of the Holy Spirit. The middle advent is likewise a sacramentally mediated event: the eyes of the two disciples on the road to Emmaus are opened when Jesus begins to celebrate Eucharist with them.

The Pentecostal hope of this middle advent is for the advent of glory and majesty, when Christ returns. His first descent was in obscurity; his final descent will be before the whole of creation, in glory, at an unknown hour. And his return is associated with judgment. The proclamation of the gospel in this in-between time functions in light of the coming judgment. Paul tells Timothy, "In the presence of God and of Christ Jesus, who is to judge the living and the dead, and in view of his appearing and his kingdom, I solemnly urge you: proclaim the message; be persistent whether the time is favorable or unfavorable; convince, rebuke, and encourage, with the utmost patience in teaching" (2 Tim 4:1–2).

What will happen at that judgment? The Bible speaks of it in images: of goats and of sheep, of pits and of fire. Does it tell of two judgments—at death and the final judgment—or only one? How final are the judgments of condemnation: eternal hell, or hellish probation? How severe is the judgment? How does Christ execute justice and mercy? What is the basis for the judgment: a confession of faith? Holiness? Orthodoxy? Orthopraxis? Christ's obedience? Our degree of participation in Christ's obedience? Whether we have followed our conscience? Answers to these questions can only be provisional and speculative, and they must be

---

4. Bernard, *In Adventu Domini*, serm. 3, 4; 5, 1, quoted in Ratzinger, *Jesus of Nazareth*, 290.

offered only with the utmost humility. What is certain is that the character of God revealed in Jesus Christ throughout his saving mysteries will be the character of God revealed at the judgment seat of Jesus Christ.

Conclusion

After Pentecost, the Spirit who dwells in Jesus Christ also dwells in those who follow him. The life he lived becomes open to us by this life-giving Gift. We pass through the middle advent as those who have been empowered to preach the good news, to confront the forces of sin and death, to bear witness to the new creation, and to live in the light of a greater hope.

Questions for Consideration

1. How may the church over the years have forgotten the role of the Holy Spirit in the life and ministry of Jesus, not to mention from the beginning of creation to final consummation?

2. Share how the Holy Spirit figures into Holy Week and into the mystery of Christ's death and resurrection.

3. In what ways is the coming or outpouring of the Holy Spirit at Pentecost the final sign of Christ's triumph before his second coming?

4. How are Pentecost and ordinary time related in the liturgical calendar and how are they key to understanding life in the "time between times"?

5. What may Charles Wesley's words "Let thy will in us be seen, done on earth as 'tis in heaven" mean to the life of the church, to the lives of Christians, in these "in-between times"?

6. How may the sacraments come into play in the life of the church during these times?

nine

Confessing Christ

What is that gospel-hope?
To be redeem'd from sin,
After his likeness to wake up,
Holy and pure within,
The Lord with all our mind
And soul and strength to love,
To lose our life for Christ, and find
A better life above.[1]

The saving mysteries of Jesus Christ—the incarnation, nativity, circumcision, baptism, fasting, temptation, agony, bloody sweat, cross, passion, resurrection, ascension, and coming of the Holy Spirit—are each and all worthy of our contemplation and devotion. In them we apprehend the revealed truth of the Father, Son, and Holy Spirit. In them we see Christ for who he really is, fully human and fully divine. But these

---

1. C. Wesley, "What Is That Gospel-Hope?," *Scripture Hymns* (1762), vol. 2, 622, stanza 1.

mysteries also call for a response: we do not merely contemplate "the Christ"; we confess that Jesus Christ is Lord.

This confession is scandalous. Nothing good comes from Nazareth, the cross is foolishness and a stumbling block, and the particularity of the confession (Jesus, the Jewish man, and no other) offends and has offended since it was first uttered. Yet we hear in Acts that "there is salvation in no one else, for there is no other name under heaven given among mortals by which we must be saved" (4:12).

More than a scandal, the confession "Jesus is Lord" is an act of worship. Thomas beholds the risen Jesus and exclaims, "My Lord and my God!" (John 20:28). This confession is a doxology, a word of praise that brings glory to the Father and that is impossible without the Holy Spirit (1 Cor 12:3). To confess the lordship of Jesus is to share in the life of the Trinity.

Still further, confessing "Jesus is Lord" is a pledge of allegiance. To say "Jesus is Lord" is also to say "Caesar is not," "Pharaoh is not," and even "I am not" the Lord. Jesus liberates us from all other lordships, for he is above all so-called lords and gods. The pledge of this confession tests all other allegiances, all other loyalties, all other commitments: do they hold up to the way of the cross? In light of this confession, every other allegiance is conditional, subject to the proviso that all must be done in subject to the superior lordship of Jesus Christ.

This confession is also therefore a call and a commitment to service. Before his betrayal, Jesus kneels before his disciples, washes their feet, and instructs them, saying, "You call me Teacher and Lord—and you are right, for that is what I am. So if I, your Lord and Teacher, have washed your feet, you also ought to wash one another's feet" (John 13:13–14). Being under the lordship of Jesus means serving as he serves us. This includes caring for fellow disciples but also caring for the world God loves. The Epistle of James reminds us that this calls us to a delicate balance, for "whoever wishes to be a friend of the world becomes an enemy of God" (4:4). Service to the world is done in light of allegiance to the Lord, never as a substitute for or an abrogation of that allegiance.

Confessing "Jesus is Lord" is a saving act. Paul tells the Romans that "if you confess with your lips that Jesus is Lord and believe in your heart that God raised him from the dead, you will be saved" (Rom 10:9). Some Christians misunderstand confession of faith in Jesus as a magical formula, as if the mere words "Jesus is Lord" were a spell, the "open sesame" that unlocks the entrance to a cave of untold treasures. The confession saves only when it bursts forth from a heart that has been filled with the Holy Spirit. It is not magic but the grace of God.

Finally, this confession is also a great commission. Jesus is first and foremost the fulfillment of Israel's hopes and expectations. Most Christians have been gentiles, not Jews, grafted onto Israel through Jesus Christ. And gentile Christians have heard of this man only because some Jews took the risk of making room for authorized versions or translations of their hopes and dreams into foreign languages and cultural forms. Jesus Christ is not the property of Western civilization. Every knee shall bow and every tongue shall confess that Jesus Christ is Lord. Jesus has condescended to respond to *Adonai, Kurios, Dominus, Herr, Lord, Señor*, so that every people, tribe, and nation can worship God in their own native tongue. But how will they hear unless someone preaches to them?

It follows that contextualized christologies are a gospel imperative. But who is Jesus? Those who would follow him are instructed to refrain from seeing him any longer "from a human point of view" (2 Cor 5:16). We believe that reflecting on the saving mysteries of Christ is an aid to that instruction. But does that mean to see Jesus through Hispanic eyes is to see him "from a human point of view"? Is it not possible to see the faces of Jesus in Asia, Africa, North America, Latin America, Europe, or Australia? These contexts can provide insights into Christ, even as we hold fast to what has been handed on to us from the apostles, the church councils, and the great teachers of the church.

A genuine Wesleyan christology depends on this confession, for the "gospel-hope" is redemption and new life for all who call upon the name of the Lord. Confessing "Jesus is Lord" is good news! In Jesus Christ, we have the perfect introduction to God. Whoever sees Jesus sees the one who sent him, God the Father. When we confess "Jesus Christ is Lord" we are claiming that we have been given access to the deep things of God. In Jesus Christ, we find the way, the truth, and the life. He is the Alpha and the Omega; he holds the whole world in his hands. Because he lives we can "lose our life for Christ" and live "a better life" also. In Jesus Christ, we have a living hope. And with John and Charles Wesley and all the company of heaven, we can sing,

> Jesus! the name high over all,
>   in hell or earth or sky;
> angels and mortals prostrate fall,
>   and devils fear and fly.

Happy, if with my latest breath
I may but gasp his name,
preach him to all and cry in death,
"Behold, behold the Lamb!"[2]

Questions for Consideration

1. What again are the saving mysteries of Christ? What other mysteries might we add?

2. How is the confession "Jesus is Lord" related to the saving mystery of Christ? That is, of what does the human response of confession consist? How is the confession of "Jesus is Lord" related to the call and commitment of a Christian? What are some of the possible dangers in such a confession?

3. If we no longer view Christ from a human point of view, how may we understand the different expressions of Christ around the world so as to further the very mission of Christ?

4. What questions may we still have about the mystery of Christ and the eight saving mysteries mentioned in this book?

5. How may Wesleyans in particular, and Christians in general, continue to sing and proclaim the mystery of God's salvation in Christ, in terms of worship, ministry, and devotion?

---

2. C. Wesley, "Jesus! the Name High over All," *United Methodist Hymnal*, No. 193, stanzas 1 and 6.

Bibliography

Anderson, Gary. "Mary in the Old Testament." *Pro Ecclesia* 16 (2007) 33–55.

Barth, Karl. *Church Dogmatics*. 4.1: *The Doctrine of Reconciliation*. Edited by G. W. Bromiley and T. F. Torrance. Edinburgh: T. & T. Clark, 1956.

Bernard of Clairvaux, Saint. *On the Song of Songs*. Translated by Killian Walsh. 4 vols. 1971–80.

The Book of Discipline of The United Methodist Church 2016. Nashville: The United Methodist Publishing House, 2016.

Bosanquet-Fletcher, Mary. "Watchwords: The Names of Christ." *Asbury Journal* 61 (2006) 13–96.

Byassee, Jason. *Trinity: The God We Don't Know*. Nashville: Abingdon, 2015.

Campbell, Ted A. *Methodist Doctrine: The Essentials*. Rev. ed. Nashville: Abingdon, 2011.

Catechism of the Catholic Church. US Catholic Church. 2nd ed. New York: Doubleday, 2012.

Cruickshank, Joanna. *Pain, Passion and Faith: Revisiting the Place of Charles Wesley in Early Methodism*. Lanham, MD: Scarecrow, 2009.

Dostoevsky, Fyodor. *The Idiot*. Translated by Alan Myers. New York: Oxford University Press, 1998.

George, Timothy. "The Blessed Virgin Mary in Evangelical Perspective." In *Mary Mother of God*, edited by Carl Braaten and Robert Jenson, 100–22. Grand Rapids: Eerdmans, 2004.

Glory to God: The Presbyterian Hymnal. Louisville: Westminster John Knox, 2013.

Guamán Poma de Ayala, Felipe. *The First New Chronicle and Good Government*. Translated and abridged by David L. Frye. Indianapolis: Hackett, 2006.

Hernaman, Claudia F. "Lord, Who Throughout These Forty Days." Hymnary.org. http://www.hymnary.org/text/lord_who_throughout_these_forty_days.

Jones, Mark. "John Calvin's Reception at the Westminster Assembly (1643–1649)." *Church History and Religious Culture* 91 (2011) 215–27.

Leith, John H., ed. *Creeds of the Churches: A Reader in Christian Doctrine from the Bible to the Present*. Atlanta: John Knox, 1982.

Maddox, Randy L. *Responsible Grace: John Wesley's Practical Theology*. Nashville: Kingswood, 1994.

Maximus the Confessor. *On the Cosmic Mystery of Jesus Christ.* Translated by Paul M. Blowers and Robert Louis Wilken. Crestwood, NY: St. Vladimir's Seminary Press, 2003.

Moltmann, Jürgen. *The Spirit of Life: A Universal Affirmation.* Translated by Margaret Kohl. Minneapolis: Fortress, 1992.

Ratzinger, Joseph. *Jesus of Nazareth.* Pt. 2, *Holy Week: From the Entrance into Jerusalem to the Resurrection.* San Francisco: Ignatius, 2011.

——. *The Spirit of the Liturgy.* Translated by John Saward. San Francisco: Ignatius, 2000.

Rejoice in the Lord: A Hymn Companion to the Scriptures. Edited by Erik Routley. Grand Rapids: Eerdmans, 1985.

Torrance, T. F. *The Trinitarian Faith: The Evangelical Theology of the Ancient Church.* 2nd ed. London: Bloomsbury, 2016.

The United Methodist Hymnal. Nashville: The United Methodist Publishing House, 1989.

Vickers, Jason. "'And We the Life of God Shall Know': Incarnation and the Trinity in Charles Wesley's Hymns." *Anglican Theological Review* 90 (2008) 329–44.

Weinandy, Thomas G. "Does God Suffer?" *First Things* 117 (2001) 35–41.

Wesley, Charles. *Charles Wesley's Published Verse.* The Center for Studies in the Wesleyan Tradition, Duke Divinity School. http://divinity.duke.edu/initiatives/cswt/charles-published-verse.

Wesley, John. *Explanatory Notes on the New Testament.* Edited by George Peck. New York: Lane and Tippett, 1845.

——. *The Works of John Wesley.* Edited by Albert C. Outler et al. Bicentennial ed. Nashville: Abingdon, 1984–.

——. *The Works of John Wesley.* Edited by Thomas Jackson. 14 vols. Reprint, Grand Rapids: Baker, 1984.

White, Thomas J. "Jesus' Cry on the Cross and His Beatific Vision." *Nova et Vetera* 5 (2007) 555–82.

Williams, Rowan. *Dostoevsky: Language, Faith, and Fiction.* The Making of the Christian Imagination. Waco: Baylor University Press, 2011. Kindle ed.

Made in United States
Orlando, FL
15 February 2024

43658900R00061